Sales Success on LinkedIn

Sales Success on LinkedIn

Using Your Existing Business Skills Online

Nevil Tynemouth

authorHOUSE®

AuthorHouse™ UK
1663 Liberty Drive
Bloomington, IN 47403 USA
www.authorhouse.co.uk
Phone: 0800.197.4150

Published by AuthorHouse   11/06/2014

ISBN: 978-1-4969-9400-4 (sc)
ISBN: 978-1-4969-9401-1 (hc)
ISBN: 978-1-4969-9402-8 (e)

Chapters

Acknowledgements

Working as part of great team is extremely important to me. Having a book on LinkedIn has come through surrounding myself with a great team. They have brought this book to life and without key people to help, I would still be playing about with some of the ideas, content and most importantly, the layout. Thanks are due to the team at New Results Training; my co-director and wife Nicola for her support, ideas and input to the book; my co director, Mike Lever, for his thoughts, challenges and support (to give a flavour of his support, after spending a couple of hours on the first edit he looked up and coined the now famous phrase "So Nevil, what is your first language because it certainly isn't English!"). Thanks to Dr Barrie Tynemouth for his editing and ideas, such as more screenshots and layout. Thanks to all others for their insights, feedback and thoughts. Collectively you have supported and shaped this book to what it is now, so it is all your fault (good or bad)!

Preface

LinkedIn has undoubtedly become an important business tool: with over 300 million users worldwide, in 20 languages and in over 200 countries worldwide (via mobile), but why do so many people join?

There are a number of different motivators:-

You might have started using LinkedIn and thought "What next?" You want to build on the basics and start using it as an effective business tool.

Lots of people have joined LinkedIn "Because everyone else has" and haven't put much thought into joining or using it as a business tool.

Others join LinkedIn because they hear about it from a number of people then get an invite from a supplier or a colleague and decide to join without being aware of how useful and effective LinkedIn can be.

Some organisations are asking all employees to create a professional profile on LinkedIn to promote a positive image to the outside world.

A handful of individuals and organisations are using LinkedIn proactively to find new potential customers, to identify important contact and to sell more of their products and services. I invite you to join this last group and increase your turnover by employing all of the techniques, tips and tools that I share in this book.

This book isn't aimed at brand new users of LinkedIn (although we will cover some of the fundamentals). I have written this on the assumption that you are already using LinkedIn, have built up some contacts and started to wonder "What do I do now....?"

I will dispel some of the myths or concerns about LinkedIn while giving you the fundamentals that will help you get the best out of it. I will share with you all of the tools and techniques we at New Results have developed and used for ourselves.

As a key starting point, it is vital that to understand that the vast majority of the skills, knowledge and behaviours you have (and use every day in face to face networking and business in general) translate easily and seamlessly to using LinkedIn effectively and efficiently. I will return to this point throughout the book, looking at individual areas with the relevant skills that translate. To help reinforce this, a useful question to ask yourself is, "If this was a face to face situation what would I do?"

Here are three examples of how face to face interactions map across to LinkedIn:-

1. How you present yourself. Before you go out to a meeting (let's say a networking meeting), you think about what to wear and what this says about you. It could be a formal suit and smart shirt or blouse. This is because we all know and have had drummed into us, that first impressions count. Because we know this, we take the time to dress

appropriately for the meeting (creative web designers might find jeans and a t-shirt represents them a little better). So what is the LinkedIn equivalent? It's your profile. More specifically, it is your profile photo. What does it say about you at first glance; does it reflect your professional appearance and is it appropriate to you and your job?

Not many people go to face to face meetings looking like this:

2. How you describe yourself in meetings. You know that point in a meeting, when you are networking or in any situation, when someone asks, "So what do you do?" How do you describe yourself and how is this reflected in your LinkedIn profile? Stop and write down how you would answer the "What do you do?" question when face to face, then look at your LinkedIn description. Is it identical? Is it near? Is it so different you aren't sure who wrote those words about you?

    Things like "Serial entrepreneur" might sound grand, but would you use this speaking to others and what does it even mean?

3. What you share and say. Before you go to a meeting with a prospective client, you usually plan some of the things you want to say and have a thought or two about how you will answer certain questions or position some of your answers. Everything you do and say in a meeting reflects on you and your organisation. Likewise, the content you put on LinkedIn and the comments and responses you

make on LinkedIn reflect on you and your organisation. The way you interact with others on LinkedIn should reflect what you do off line. The simple thing to remember is if you wouldn't say it face to face then you shouldn't put in online (LinkedIn or elsewhere).

With these three areas in mind I have a clear idea of the approach I take when using LinkedIn. I will keep referring to this concept of what you do face to face and what you do on LinkedIn. It works for me, it works for others we train and we know if you take the same approach, it will work for you.

The LinkedIn Process to Success

This book started with us (as a business) learning how to use LinkedIn and then making it work for us: from building our profile, marketing our proposition and ultimately winning clients. Naturally we have made some mistakes along the way, but we have learned from them and produced techniques that proved to be very effective. These techniques have helped us in finding new customers and generating new revenues. Some of our clients had also approached us, wanting to learn more about LinkedIn; they asked us to write a training course about it for them. Using what we already knew and were applying ourselves, we started researching what was worthwhile knowing, understanding and using on LinkedIn. When we pulled all the material together, we had around three full days of training content (far more than the client needed). So we decided to use the core of this material to run one day training courses and to coach clients on the most effective ways to use LinkedIn for them and to help them meet their own business aims.

I have shared all of our experience, ideas, research and results in this book to provide you with a practical tool that you can use immediately. Like us, you can expect to generate more business, get more contacts and find new potential customers.

Where to start?

Well it's worth starting with LinkedIn as an organisation and understanding what they do. LinkedIn's company mission statement is to: "Connect the world's professionals to make them more productive and successful."

If you think about this in relation to our approach described in our introduction of converting your current skills and abilities to online ability on LinkedIn, this sits very well. Business (like life) is all about making and retaining great connections and relationships. This approach is fundamental to all businesses; you need to develop and build the best relationships with customers, suppliers and employees. LinkedIn can help you do this in a time effective way and opens up additional possibilities for the face to face and other online relationships you have (Facebook, twitter etc.)

Malcom Gladwell's The Tipping Point gives a full explanation of how important those relationships and connections are. He talks about the importance of different types of relationships in business

"There are exceptional people out there who are capable of starting epidemics. All you have to do is find them."

"Acquaintances, in sort, represent a source of social power, and the more acquaintances you have the more powerful you are."

"The values of the world we inhabit and the people we surround ourselves with have a profound effect on who we are."

Malcolm Gladwell, The Tipping Point

These are the fundamental principles we are looking to emulate online.

LinkedIn's company slogan is: "Relationship Matters". How fitting and apt in the context of this book. If you are an employee or run your own company, one thing that you can be certain of is that "relationship matters". Whether that relationship is with fellow company directors, employees, suppliers, business contacts or customers, they all matter to you and your business. Get these relationships right and you have a powerful key to unlocking business and personal success.

I spend a lot of time talking to our clients about how they conduct their on and offline approach to relationships; I will share their many tips and thoughts through this book. The one big factor that comes out time and again with relationships is listening. I passionately believe that everyone can improve their listening, how they listen, why they listen, when they listen, who they listen to and what to listen for. If you are interested in enhancing your own listening skills then a fine place to start is TED talks. This online community and collection of great speakers has a wealth of useful information. Take some time to watch Julian Treasure: "5 ways to listen better" and Ernesto Sirolli's: "Want to help someone? Shut up and listen!"

Plenty of business develops out of conversations and the most effective individuals in those conversations are those who can listen. Those who listen spot opportunities, identify issues, understand situations and can gain an in-depth knowledge that allows business to take place. The approach I promote for success on LinkedIn is exactly the same: communication with the emphasis on listening.

LinkedIn is part of the new wave of social media and many users (as commentators have pointed out) get lost in one way traffic; talking but not listening, posting but not interacting, shouting but not listening. Face to face, these approaches do not work, just imagine this meeting:

Someone walks into a bustling networking event with 25 successful business people. They start telling everyone how great their products and services are. They go on telling the group how great their products and services are and how the group really should buy them. They do all of this without listening to what people are talking about. They don't interact to responses or conversations: they just talk at people. You can probably guess how many of the 25 want to interact, never mind buy from them. I hope you haven't been to too many meetings like that (although I must admit one or two do come to mind) it's no surprise that this approach doesn't work face to face, and yet for some it is a revelation that it doesn't work online either. In all environments, the fundamentals apply. You need to engage people in a conversation; you need to interact with people and you need to share information that others will find interesting and useful (whether online or offline).

This book is going to show you how to refine and apply your current skills in a new way that will grow your relationships, help you to connect with other professionals and make you more successful.

Nevil Tynemouth

This is the original rough drawing for the model we use ourselves and helped many others use too. You can see (very clearly) that it isn't a linear process. While it works in practice, it does make it difficult to lay all this information out in a series of linear chapters. But that's okay. It's your book, so feel free to chop around and dive into the chapters as you see fit. I have provided links between chapters and refer to parts of the process and how they link to each other.

I'll guide you through the original model, and much more.

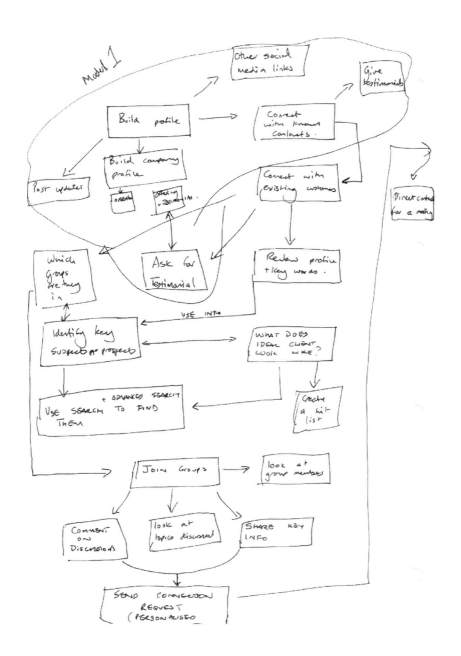

CHAPTER 1

Understanding why YOU use LinkedIn

The world is shrinking, not physically (clearly as my drive to work hasn't got any shorter), but in a connected world way. A greater personal and business network across the world based on technology means our relationships and network is being condensed with more connections, data and information at our fingertips. As an example, how many of us have "contacts" in countries we've never visited? Think about this in a number of ways.

How far do you travel for meetings now? How long will you sit in your car in a train or on a plane for an important meeting, conference or appointment? The technology we take for granted today has helped speed up the whole process of shrinking our world. Round the world yachtsmen and women have satellite phones; explorers can tweet from the North Pole or the top of Mount Everest. We can send and receive our messages, keeping

1

in contact with our whole network whenever and from wherever we want.

The idea of a shrinking world was hypothesised after World War One when reconstruction work started to look at the social interaction of larger groups of people. Considerable time and effort was put into looking at the make-up of both commercial and residential areas to understand how people would use them while interacting with others. The telegraph, phone line, mobile phones and email have all increased the pace of change and the availability of our network. Gone are the days of booking an international call or sending a letter and waiting for a response. More than ever, more of us now have the world at our fingertips.

How does this relate to our work on LinkedIn and how we use it?

Let's start with the 6 degrees of separation (or Kevin Bacon, for those under the age of 40). The six degrees of separation is a very simple concept: you are no more than 6 steps away from anyone else on the planet. You know someone who knows someone who knows someone who knows someone who knows someone who knows Barack Obama or Jay Z, or if you must, Kevin Bacon. In reality, whenever we test this we now find that people are much more closely connected and we find that the number of steps is far less than 6.

In recent examples with different groups, we set out to understand how many steps separated individuals in these groups from HRH the Queen. The results really shocked us: less than two steps! In each case, the two individuals knew someone who was closely connected to the Queen. We don't often reflect on how well connected we and those around us are. I wonder if you started with a contact in mind and worked this through for yourself, how many steps would you be from a key contact or a famous person you would like to work with?

This is all lovely, but so far all you have is a parlour game or something to mull over with your colleagues on a "busy" Friday afternoon.

Simply by combining LinkedIn and the 6 degrees way, we need to start thinking about your network; who you currently know. Rather than technology, keep it simple and start with a pen and blank sheet of paper (usually a glass of wine helps too, assuming this is at home on an evening, not in the office on a Monday morning!) Draw up some lists of names under the following headings:

Who do I currently work with?
Who did I work with in the past?
Who are my customers?
Who are my business (including networking) contacts?
Who are my friends and family?

How strong is your network?

Now let's be really mean. Let's assume you aren't a terribly well networked person and you only have 10 names in each list and out of each list of 10, only 5 are on LinkedIn. So you now have 25 people that you can (potentially) connect with on LinkedIn. Let's assume they are in a similar position to you and each has only 25 unique contacts. By connecting up with these 25 people you now are a second degree connection to 625 people and a third degree connection to 15,625 people (again, assuming your second degree contacts each has only 25 unique contacts).

This is the power of the spider's web of networking that is LinkedIn, in reality, I bet you have far more than 25 names on your lists (200+ is a reasonable guess). I bet more than 50% of those people are on LinkedIn and I bet they each have far more than 25 connections. Just for fun, the numbers (if you get 150 connections and assuming they all have the same), would yield 22,500 second degree connections and 3,375,000 third degree connections. Over 3 million third degree connections! Now the only flaw in our logic is we have assumed that these are all new, separate and unique connections. In reality, if you connect to 20 of the people you currently work with then chances are that 19 of THEIR connections will be the co-workers that you both share. Having said that, even taking out the duplicates, you can really start to see how the power of 6 degrees of separation on LinkedIn is a powerful tool for you.

Starting with our sheet of paper we can now set to work on growing our network on LinkedIn.

You can connect with people quickly and simply on LinkedIn. Fortunately LinkedIn has some simple and powerful tools to help us do just that. I will put some words of warning in here though. Just because something is easy doesn't always mean it will be effective. The built in, simple tools you can use will reach out to a large number of your connections very quickly, but with that speed of automation you risk losing some of your personal touch. These tools include the email connection tool that LinkedIn provides. It does this by accessing your email contacts directly from your email account and sending out mass contact requests. These bulk approaches just use the standard connection request message – "I'd like to add you to my professional network on LinkedIn." There is lots more on how important this message is in Chapter 3.

So LinkedIn will allow you to connect up with the list you have created. Assuming you are an averagely well-connected individual, you can have up to 250 connections in a relatively short period of time. Great! Or a more likely thought at this point might be, so what? Connections are only of use if you have a clear idea and strategy on why are you are using LinkedIn. This might sound like a strange point, but LinkedIn gets used by individuals and organisations in a range of ways.

Understanding why you use LinkedIn and what you are trying to achieve.

So here is the big question you need to ask yourself:

What do I want to use LinkedIn for?

- Is it part of my sales and marketing plan?
- Is it about finding new customers? Suppliers?
- Keeping tabs on my competitors?
- Increasing my knowledge and skills?
- Keeping pace with my own market?
- A content marketing tool?
- Raising my profile?
- Looking for a new job?

It is worth investing time now, to give yourself the opportunity to understand what you want to use LinkedIn for. Our advice for you is to write it down somewhere safe, email it to yourself or keep it somewhere so you can refer back to it, either as a reminder or to edit over time. To help you with this, we have provided some space at the end of the chapter to fill in your reason for using LinkedIn. It is always a handy little check throughout your work on LinkedIn. Look at what you are doing and look at what you are trying to achieve. Are they aligned; is there a clear link or are you just messing about and killing time (very easy to do on LinkedIn)? Have a goal and work towards it. Simple stuff, but more people would benefit from doing this. Think about the time you invest in any sort of business activity; you need to know what you are trying to achieve and critically, when (or if) you have achieved it!

In this respect, LinkedIn is no different to any other aspect of your business. Start with the end in mind. Sketch out now what you want to achieve from LinkedIn. Once you set yourself a clear goal you can takes steps towards it, knowing, with each step, what your success looks like. You will also understand what you can review along the way to see that you are on track.

With this new goal in mind you might find yourself dotting about the chapters in this book, and that's fine. I wrote it with you in mind! You saw from the diagram of the original LinkedIn process that this wasn't a step by step process, or a set of things to do. It's not a tick list of things to achieve. Whenever we train, coach or work side by side with people we always have to move around LinkedIn in the way they want and in a way that moves them towards their goals. We would encourage you to do the same.

Let's look at some of the areas often identified as ways to use LinkedIn in a little more detail:

Is it part of my sales and marketing plan?

LinkedIn should be an integrated part of your holistic marketing plan (not a stand-alone approach); it consolidates your online and offline marketing and aligns with all of your other marketing. Your marketing messages online (in every place) should integrate with your blogs (and other social media) representing you and your organisation. This online approach needs to reflect your overall sales and marketing approach. If I look at your website, your sales and marketing collateral or listen to you at a networking event I should be able to see and hear some consistent language and approach across everything you do. It's all part of your brand and a consistent brand message helps others understand you and what you have to offer much more effectively than a set of disparate approaches and messages.

Is it about finding new customers? Suppliers?

Lots of people we work with are looking to grow the number of customers they have. If I am honest, they generally want more sales and this is slightly different. Let me explain why. Lots of your current customers won't know everything that you currently do and offer! It's a fact of life and as you are reading this, you are probably thinking, well that doesn't apply to me. Trust me on this, clients are just like you and I, they don't always listen, they forget and unsurprisingly they have a lot of other things to think about on their own to do list. They don't normally have you at the top of their list. Many organisations can grow sales significantly just by getting a consistent message out to all of their existing customers. So using LinkedIn helps you get your message out to your existing customers as well as helping you find new customers. Either way, you can grow your business using LinkedIn. Finding suppliers or new potential customers on LinkedIn is a great time saver; you can see what they do, their experience and who they have worked with, as well as seeing recommendations from existing customers. What a great thing to do: save time and find the right suppliers to help your business thrive. Probably the most significant request we get when working with people on LinkedIn is to grow their business and find new clients. We and our clients have found LinkedIn a great place to do this and we will dedicate a significant part of this book to showing you how to do this.

Keeping tabs on my competitors?

Want to do some research? Want to find out what particular companies or individuals are up to? Want to snoop around? All of this information and more is available at your fingertips on LinkedIn. Have a look at chapter 8 on how to use the search tool effectively to find the individuals and information you want.

Increasing my knowledge and skills?

There is a plethora of information uploaded to LinkedIn every single day that is useful to you in your business today. No matter what industry you work in there are online groups that will help you get more information, insight and advice to help you grow your knowledge and skills. LinkedIn has key influencers sharing their own insights and ideas freely with others. These influencers include Richard Branson, Deepak Chopra, Jack Welch, and Bill Gates. These are the heavy hitters that, given the chance, you would probably want to sit down and listen to.

Keeping pace with my own market?

We have already discussed the shrinking world concept and the fact that the information we have access to is growing at an exponential rate. As an example, we now do more business globally in one day than in the full year of 1950. How do you filter this and how do you ensure that you don't miss the important points? LinkedIn can be the solution to keep this information coming to you and keeping you up to date. We will discuss this in detail in chapters on groups and sharing information. A simple starting point is following the key influencers in your market place and looking at the information that they share.

A content marketing tool?

Content marketing and industry thought leadership are becoming increasingly important tools for attracting new customers. It is through the use of great, new, useful and engaging content that you can attract and retain an audience. LinkedIn has changed over time to accommodate this shift and allow great content marketing to happen, giving you the tools to run simple a campaign from your desk without the need for previous knowledge or experience. We will explore the concept of content marketing and thought leadership throughout the book.

Raising your profile?

Very often people use LinkedIn to become more visible. This may be in order to raise their visibility with customers or within their own marketplace. Raising your profile can be used as an inbound technique – the more people know me, the more people will ask and engage with me. Or it can be used as a reference point, for example when a client or supplier "checks me out" before or after a meeting to ensure I present a credible and effective online presence. How often do you "google" someone before you meet them for the first time? Guess what? They're "googling" you too, so it's imperative to have a profile that's saying the right things for you! It's also worth noting that LinkedIn is often the first search results when you google an individual's name, so it's often the first port of call when researching a business contact.

Looking for a job?

Lots of people think this is the primary purpose of LinkedIn – "Oh isn't that the place where you put your CV online?" (I still hear this a lot). It is a great place to look for a new job and also be found as the perfect potential employee. The more work you do in polishing your profile, the more people will notice and find you. I often encourage clients to look for and research potential new recruits on LinkedIn, but this book isn't aimed at those looking to recruit using LinkedIn. There are already some great books out there that do that. The general principals and ideas we discuss will help you raise your profile and employability and will help others to find you when they are looking to recruit.

If you have not already done so, take some time now and list the reasons why you want to use LinkedIn, including what you want to achieve. If you aren't yet sure then why not read the rest of this book, get some inspiration and come back to this point. If you already have a clear idea of what you want to achieve, then read on! The rest of the book will give you the skills you need to achieve your goals.

What do I want to use Linked In for?

CHAPTER 2

Creating a brilliant LinkedIn profile

What makes one individual interesting and engaging and another one less so? Your mind will decide this very easily and subconsciously for you when you are meeting people face to face: You may have found yourself scanning a room and identifying one or two people you would like to speak to and one or two you might want to avoid. That is you looking out at others. Now consider that they are performing the same filtering process when they look at you. Do you want to be on the list they want to engage with or the list of people they want to avoid? Self-explanatory really, but in order to attract people in we must think about how we appear attractive (I mean this in the business context: this isn't dating advice, but if you find it useful to think that way, then some very similar principals apply).

Your profile on LinkedIn will help attract people in (especially when they are scanning through a group). It seems obvious then, that dedicating time to getting your profile right is extremely important. That's why we are here at the start of the book, getting the fundamentals on LinkedIn absolutely right. Don't skip this chapter if you already have a profile (even a very good profile) as 99.5% of people we work with and review their profile find at least one thing new. The vast majority find a whole range of improvements we can make to give them (and now you) a great and engaging and effective profile.

Ask yourself a few questions before we start:

- What makes someone compelling to talk to at a networking event?
- What do you look for in people when you go to an exhibition?
- How do you choose who to speak to at the events you attend?

In answering some of these questions I wonder how many of the following words came up?

> Boring, uninteresting, plain, quiet, shy, understated, badly dressed, introverted people.

If you are at an event you generally keep away from these sorts of people. You look for someone you can have a conversation with, engage with and someone who interests you. This principal applies directly to LinkedIn. Imagine your profile is a representation of you in an online networking event and all the others on LinkedIn are at the same networking event.

Ask yourself a question, would you describe your LinkedIn profile with any of these words?

> Boring, uninteresting, plain, quiet, shy, understated, badly dressed, introverted.

Would others use any of these words to describe your profile on LinkedIn?

Time to get stuck in and build a powerful and engaging profile!

A great profile is by far the most significant part to your work on LinkedIn. In answering the three questions we posed, you started to think about how you build relationships and find connections in a face to face environment. With this in mind, you can build your profile and do all of the other things we describe throughout the book. If you haven't got your profile as good as it can be, the other things we describe might not have as much impact as possible. The profile is an area to dedicate some time to, both as an initial piece of work and then ongoing, refreshing the information and keeping your profile bang up to date.

Let's get this clear and straight. Your profile **is** your first impression, when I find you (and I **will** find you) online, what initial impression does your LinkedIn profile give me?

NOTE: to edit your profile, simply hover over the profile option on the home menu on LinkedIn and two drop down menus appear. The first is "Edit Profile", simply click on this link. This will open your profile with a series of little blue pens next to each area you can edit.

Let's start at the very top:

Profile Photo

Your photo - this is the part that will grab the attention of the "visual" people who find your profile, and LinkedIn's own research (See below *) confirms the fact that your profile picture is key in your profile. It is the first thing that people will notice when they land on your profile page. All of the work we have done on LinkedIn points to the fact that people expect a good quality, business style picture. Now let's be clear - I am not the most photogenic person going, but I did choose to stack the odds in my favour. I invested a small amount of money in a professional photographer (Thanks Angela Carrington and Andy Ragsdale) and use a good quality image on my profile. Let's look at some of the alternatives to a professional photo:

- A good quality photo taken by a friend. Get the best camera you can, get the friend who takes the best photos and spend some time on getting it right.
- A cropped photo that you like. This can work if you have had some great photos taken in the past (recent past please not 20 years ago).
- A nice holiday snap of you. A personal point, but the vast majority of people I speak to (80% upwards I would estimate) indicate that a holiday photo puts them off slightly. So if you are Richard Branson or Alan Sugar and you can afford to lose potential clients then yes by all means use a holiday photo. If you want to maximise your chances then let's leave this option.
- A selfie. Really? Really? Just no. This isn't Facebook.

> * According to LinkedIn's own blog "Professionals that add a photo are seven times more likely to have their LinkedIn Profile viewed in general than people who don't have a photo. http://blog.linkedin.com/2011/11/18/linkedin-drdrew/

A couple of other things to note about the photo:

- A larger file size and quality will allow users to get a larger picture of you by clicking on the magnifying glass at the bottom right of your profile picture.
- Think about the background and surroundings; we see the odd thing in the background that spoils an otherwise great photo.
- Is black and white or colour best for you? (I alternate between both).
- Keeping your photo up to date is a must. That photo of you in your youth might be great, but when people meet you in real life (20 years after the photo was taken) it can throw people

Lots of people will notice your profile photo before they get to any of the carefully crafted words that you put on LinkedIn. Get a picture that people will notice, its as simple as that.

> NOTE – LinkedIn's own terms say that you need to have a photo of a person on your personal profile, not a logo or a graphic.

Key words (your headline)

Next let's look at the part of the profile that has a great deal of impact, as it is the first thing (alongside the photo) that other users will notice. It is your name and your description of yourself. LinkedIn calls this your headline and this is a great way to think about it. Newspapers use headlines to grab people's attention and use words and phrases that make readers want to read on and find out more.

Imagine a newspaper headline that read "Stuff happened" or "Someone does something". It might make you laugh, but it wouldn't really drag you in to read on. Is this what your headline is doing, causing people to just sail past without paying you some attention? Have you got a headline that makes people stop and then find out more?

Take some time over your headline and follow the broad principles used in news headlines. Make it interesting, accurate and leave them wanting more. So here are the things to avoid.

- Don't just put your job title (that goes in further down on your profile).
- Don't put your company name (you put that further down your profile).
- Don't waste any of the space that you are given.
- Don't use capitals (NO NEED TO SHOUT).

What do you put in then? Well, time to think like potential customers (or those you are trying to raise your profile with). What would they search for, what words would they like to hear, what things would create a level of curiosity?

Think about what you do for customers, particularly what the result or output is, what you do to help other individuals or companies. This is the information that potential customers trawling LinkedIn want to see. This is an approach that I have found can be very powerful way to grow your business on and offline. Help your customers by making things easy for them. Focus on what is important for them and consider their perspective and point of view fully. If you apply this to your LinkedIn profile you can describe what you do to help customers, what effect you can have, what value you add for them and what they will get when working with you. This puts you in a customer centric place and starts to make you attractive to potential clients.

EXAMPLE: Would you use "Experienced marketing professional" OR "Growing your new customers through online and traditional marketing, from social media to print and design"?

The second example is simple in the fact it explains more about what you can do for me or potential customers, it describes, in simple language what I will get from you and what you do. In short I can easily understand you as a person and see how you might work with me and my business.

Now, have a look at the way you describe yourself on LinkedIn in this section. Log into your account and look at the words you use to describe yourself just below your name. Most people have "Sales Director at ABC Corp" or "Manager at PQY restaurants" or "Owner at My Business". Now in essence that seems to make sense, a short simple description of what you do. But when you think about it you list this title, company and a detailed description in the "Experience" section. So what else can you use this section for? Well you could think like your potential customers (and key contacts) and put some words in there that your customers might search for.

An example of this was the profile of one of the great people we work with, Dr Simon Raybould (uk.linkedin.com/pub/simonraybould/0/36/321), who is a fantastic specialist trainer for presentations and public speaking. When we first looked at his profile, he had missed out the words "public speaking" from his profile. This meant when we did a geographic search (more on

17

advanced search in chapter 6) for public speaking, he didn't appear in the search results. This meant he was hard to find. Despite being a fantastic public speaker, any contact or potential customer couldn't find him. It only took a few seconds to put this right and now he can easily be found on LinkedIn.

In addition, eye tracking studies further reveal that an individual's photo and headline are the two most viewed elements on a LinkedIn profile page.
http://mashable.com/2011/11/30/social-profile-eye-tracking/#36359LinkedIn

Location and industry

The next part is a simple case of ensuring you have the right location and main industry selected. It is surprising how many people still have an old location or main industry (usually based on a previous job). Simply edit your profile and select the most appropriate main industry from the pre-determined list that LinkedIn have created, then select your specific location.

Getting this part of your profile absolutely the best it can be is simply the most important thing you can do. Even some simple changes and a very short time on refining these key points have been shown, time and time again, to have a positive effect on what you can get from LinkedIn.

Your Contact Details

This is a drop down section with a little file icon just below the number of contacts you currently have. This often gets missed out or is out of date. We regularly see individuals who show their old company or previous employer's website, twitter link or telephone number. That's like handing out an out of date business card when networking. Not the best way of growing business or showing you are organised.

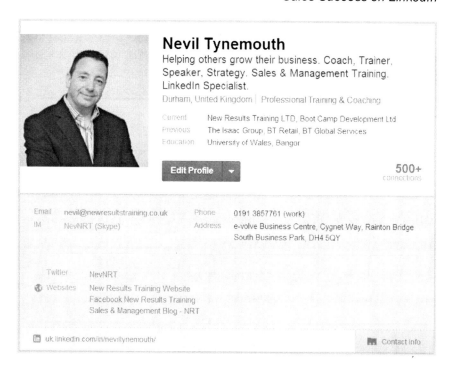

Think in terms of the business card that you use when you meet people or go networking. Is it blank? Probably not - you probably put all sorts of information on there; your website, mobile and office number, twitter and Facebook details, address etc. LinkedIn allows you to do this and more. And the great news is this is underused by most people, so get ahead of the game and fill all of these details in.

People can see these contact details when they view your profile by clicking on the small filing card icon next to the word contact. So make sure all of the information on there is up to date and you are happy to share with other LinkedIn users (it is amazing how many people have their personal mobile number or email address still listed there).

Email, phone number and address are straight forward. If you tweet make sure your twitter name / handle is on there. Then LinkedIn gives you up to three web addresses or URL's you can post. I currently have a link to our company website, Facebook page and blog. I have also customised the names to ensure that anyone who looks at any of these is clear about where they are heading.

Lastly in your contact information is your public profile URL (see the image below to find it!). This is the link that you can publish on your email footer, on your business card or in documents and proposals you produce that takes people straight to your profile. If you haven't done anything with this before, your profile URL will be a mix of your name and a random set of numbers and characters. To make this a bit neater, simply click on the edit icon and select a new URL you would like (usually your name or an abbreviation of). If you have a name others share (I NEVER have this problem), then you might need to tweak the URL you choose to select one that someone else hasn't grabbed. LinkedIn will advise you whether the URL you have chosen is available.

uk.linkedin.com/in/neviltynemouth/

Summary

All of this work so far is focussed on making you easy to get to know and looking more professional. Think of that in a face to face sense, the people you meet. Some are very easy to talk to and are very engaging. Others can feel like pulling teeth when you are trying to engage them in any sort of meaningful conversation. LinkedIn isn't (quite) a conversation, but you can make yourself easy to get to know by applying all of these techniques and laying out all of the information you present in a simple and effective way. After all, doesn't it look more professional if all of your details are up to date and are there to be found?

Now let's imagine you have had a brief meeting with a potential contact face to face and you decide to arrange a separate meeting to start to get to know each other a little better. The rest of your profile page is the equivalent of this meeting, it is providing the detail, the in-depth information and background around who you are, what you do and details of your work experience.

The first paragraph is a summary of all of these things, it's a top level review of you (think "Executive Summary"), how you help people, what you do and your experience. Use simple language and invite curiosity to draw people in to find out more either by reading on or contacting you directly. You can also embed video into this section. If you haven't got an introduction video I would highly recommend getting one (or some). Videos are a great way of getting lots of information over in a short space of time. You come to life and people can see and hear you speak some of the words you have laid out in your profile. That is a powerful way of engaging a lot of the viewers of your profile.

Experience

Next comes the in-depth detail on your current and previous jobs, an engaging look at the specific work, results and achievements made in each of your roles (LinkedIn put this under the heading of "Experience").

List all of your current positions; lots of people have multiple positions either as a director, employee, volunteer, etc. Make sure you capture and list all of your current roles. List your correct job title and then provide a brief and punchy description. Think about what you want to say and consider including some of the following areas:

- Main purpose of your role.
- Results and outcomes of what you do.
- Facts and figures, results shout louder than a detailed description.
- Areas you have developed or created.
- Innovative and different ways you work.
- Awards and recognition received in each role.
- Key achievements.
- Notable accomplishments.
- Main areas of experience and skills.

Once you have completed this for your current role(s) it is a simple case of going through your career and listing all of your previous companies or jobs and providing a similar level of detail. Some people love to look through this detail to see where you have come from and what you have done. Don't be shy and hide these things, let's get them all listed down.

Having all of your current and previous jobs listed with an effective and punchy description really helps to engage people and provides a great level of information to start those great discussions.

Now let's look at a few of the more detailed areas that some viewers of your profile can find very useful.

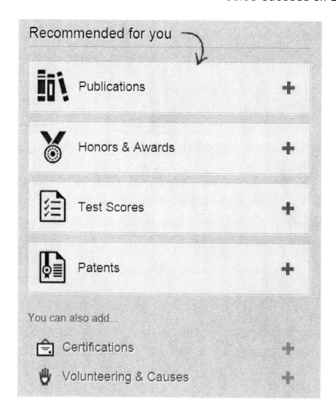

Projects

This is a great tool to highlight current projects either within your organisation or those that involve multiple contacts from various organisations. You can simply add a project to your profile, provide a description and some of the details to engage your audience. You can tag other people into this project and in doing so it will appear on their profiles as well (once they click on the automatically generated invitation). This simple tool can help to raise the profile of what you are currently working on and recognise others that have an input.

Then there are a whole range of areas to add in as additional information toward the bottom of your profile. This is the real "nitty gritty" of who you are and what you do. It gives you the opportunity to show some of the additional areas you are involved with.

Let's look at each area individually (not all will apply, simply select the ones that do and fill in the details!):

All of these areas give your profile viewers that deeper and greater insight to you as an individual. It can add credibility and depth to what you do. Some people viewing your profile will want to find as much about you as possible before they decide to connect or contact you. Make their life easy, invest a small amount of time getting these sections completed.

Courses

List all of the (relevant) courses you have completed. (Your cycling proficiency and 25m swimming award should be left off).

Languages

For those fortunate enough to be able to speak a range of languages, here is your opportunity to highlight what languages you can speak and to what level.

Publications

List all of your white papers, eBooks or books here. This can be used a simple promotional tool for any publication you have been involved with.

Organisations

What other organisations are you involved with and what do you do for them (lots of people have lots of interests and involvement outside of their day job, but don't always tell others about this).

Honors (American spelling) and awards

What other achievements do you want to highlight (still no room for the cycling proficiency).

Test scores

Where appropriate, relevant test scores can be uploaded.

Patents

What a great thing to highlight, patents you have developed or own.

Volunteering and causes

List all of the causes, charities and organisations you support.

All of these areas are a great way of giving an in-depth level of detail and can help others find common ground for starting a conversation. When you meet people face to face you search for this common ground (sameness) and by providing this information on LinkedIn, you can help others find the common ground to have a conversation with you. Invest a little time to get this information on your profile:

I cannot stress how important this area is. Getting your profile to an excellent standard is the key to using LinkedIn successfully.

The more appealing your profile, the more likely people are to accept your invitation to connect or on viewing you fantastic profile, they are more likely to send you a connection request. Whatever activity you undertake on LinkedIn, people will look at your profile, they will make a judgement on how much effort you have put into your profile and how complete it is.

LinkedIn provides some excellent and simple to use tools to help you to improve your profile. You will either get a large blue box at the top of your profile where updates or gaps in your profile are highlighted. You may also get a "complete my profile" button to the right of your picture. Clicking this will take you to a stage by stage set of questions and ideas to prompt you to complete all areas of your profile.

On the right hand side, LinkedIn also shows a simple circular graphic on how complete your profile is and it gives a rating, right the way up to "All-star" for those who have completed your profile. Just below this there is a simple click through where you can share your newly updated profile (and at any other time you like) via your Twitter or Facebook accounts, if you have these connected to LinkedIn. It creates a standard message, but you can personalise this for your own audience.

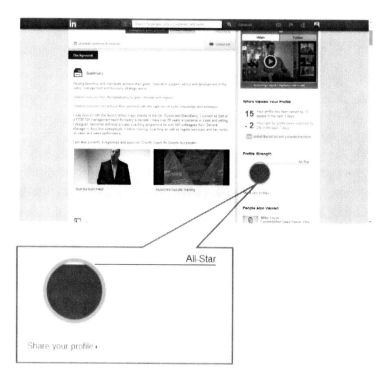

Helpful areas to get the most from your profile page:

People You May Know

Sticking to the right hand side of your profile there are a number of different areas worth looking at. LinkedIn suggests (in a couple of places) people you might know. This is based on your current connections and likely second degree connections. It can be worth looking through this list and connecting with those that you know and would like to link with.

Who's Viewed Your Profile

Again on the right is the "who's viewed my profile" (also available from the profile menu at the top of any page on LinkedIn). We touch on this in a couple of places through the book and it can be used for a number of things. Have a look now and see who has been looking at your profile.

People Also Viewed

Further down the right hand side of your profile you can see the "People Also Viewed" list. These are the profiles that others will have moved on to after browsing your profile. It is worthwhile seeing who else your profile viewers are looking at. It could be your colleagues or competitors in this list. It is worth thinking about why they looked at others: - are they looking around at some alternatives (you and your competitors) for some new products and services?

Having a fantastic profile isn't a one-time piece of work. Take some time to keep it up to date, change you profile picture, update your experience add in new relevant information. Make this part of your ongoing work on LinkedIn. We all like interesting and dynamic people, make your self interesting and dynamic on LinkedIn by keeping your new fantastic profile bang up to date. People buy from people they know, like and trust. Become a person others would like to know, like and trust via your LinkedIn profile, mirror your offline capabilities and work with a great approach to your own LinkedIn profile. No one can sell you better than you can yourself. Invest a good amount of time in building an honest, not a modest LinkedIn profile.

Why have a profile like this:

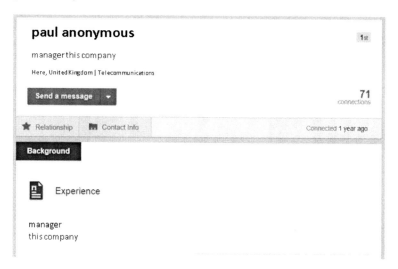

When you can have a profile that looks like one of these?

Mike Lever

Current British Sales Trainer of the Year. Management Development & Sales Training. Coaching and Business Strategy

Durham, United Kingdom | Professional Training & Coaching

Current	New Results Training Ltd, Sales Boot Camp UK
Previous	Northern Rock Plc, Sales Contact Centre, Newcastle Area
Education	Institute of Financial Services

Send a message ▾

500+
connections

Background

 Summary

Involved in training & coaching for over 20 years. I'm fortunate that my job is my passion.

At New Results Training we help individuals and businesses to increase their performance, by:

☐ Working together to design and deliver your growth strategy. We're accredited to the Coaching for Growth programme.

☐ 1:1 coaching – clients include Group Chairman. We're Practitioner Licensees of Lifestyle Architecture.

☐ Enhancing your customers' experience of you and your business. We help you to understand the full customer journey, including when first impressions really form and what it means for your turnover.

☐ Improving sales performance and sales capacity by causing your sales team to think & behave 'customer first'.

☐ Creating and delivering sales training – for SMEs, local Government bodies and Multinational Corporations – that work on knowledge, skills and behaviours. Our clients' feedback is that our approach causes margins and turnover to increase.

☐ Working with you to design and implement tools that maintain the desired staff performance.

BESMA2013
The British Excellence in Sales & Marketing Awards
SALES TRAINER OF THE YEAR
WINNER

Call 0800 030 4323 to discuss how we can help you

Britain's Sales Trainer of the Year 2013-14

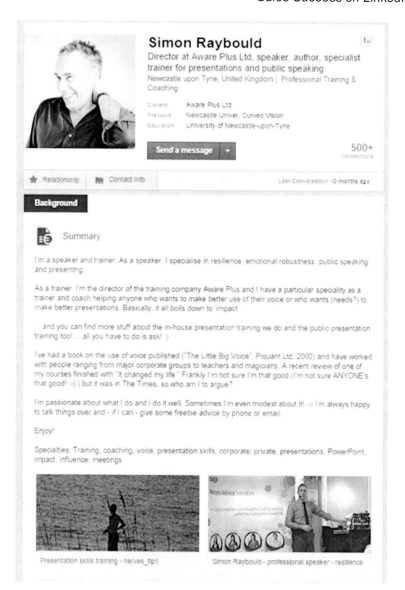

Note: - We have provided a simple checklist at the end of the book to help you get the best possible profile.

CHAPTER 3

Building your online contacts and network

Think about the most successful people you know and respect in a business setting. Many of these people will be extremely well connected, always know the "right person". They will often have a group of trusted people they can go to with any issues, ideas or opportunities. You can model these people and replicate what they do on and off line. LinkedIn can be a reflection of how well you can build a network of appropriate contacts around you.

To do this, it is all about focussing on your specific LinkedIn goals (think about the questions you answered in Chapter 1) and being clear about what you want to achieve. This is transferring your business growth approach off line to your approach on LinkedIn.

The first question we need to ask is:

Why are you building your online network?

Is it to raise your profile, find customers, be found by others or find a new job?

Always work with your goals in mind and move towards them. If you aren't sure about what you are doing, stop and ask if what you are doing on LinkedIn is moving you towards your goal. It's very easy to get distracted (especially on a great in-depth tool like LinkedIn). Equally your goals may change over time. Look at what you are trying to achieve and what activity you are undertaking. Are they aligned?

With all of that in mind, let's look at a series of ideas to grow your connections and online network (after all the vast majority of people are trying to build that powerful online set of connections to help them achieve their business goals).

This starts off with an argument about two very different approaches and I want to be crystal clear about this, I am going to sit on the fence on this one. The argument is based around whether you should connect with everyone and anyone on LinkedIn or should you be selective? In all of the work we have done in training, development, researching and working with teams and individuals on LinkedIn, there are two distinct camps. What I would like to do is point out the two camps to you and let you make the decision on the basis of what is right for you.

The first camp says I will only connect with people I know, I have met or have some sort of relationship with. As you meet people face to face, work with customers and develop relationships with suppliers you will connect with them on LinkedIn. This means that LinkedIn will reflect what you do day to day in your business. This creates a concentrated list of very specific and tangible and close connections.

For each of the two options I would like to give a balanced view, so let's see what is for and against this accepting all connection requests:

Pros:

- You KNOW them, so you can pick the phone up and speak to them or interact with them in a meaningful way on LinkedIn
- A smaller, tighter number of connections focusses you on specific areas of work and shows the world your focus and what is important to you
- Less spam, less selling and less "finding out" from distant connections
- You can easily manage (see later chapters) and market to small specific groups
- Easier to communicate with tight focussed groups

Cons:

- Less people see your marketing and sales messages
- Less reach (think 6 degrees of separation)
- Potentially less interaction from a smaller group
- Less (general) information coming in to you
- Smaller digital footprint

The second camp takes the completely opposite approach and **says that I seek to make as many connections as possible.** It takes all of the work described above and adds in as many others as possible. The only exceptions to this would be obvious spammers or false accounts, but other than these few exceptions, this approach relies on connecting with and making as many online connections on LinkedIn as possible.

Pros:

- Creates a large pool of connections for sales and marketing information
- Raises your profile with a wider group
- Lots of "loose" connections to help you find people and help you to be found
- Greater diversity of information coming in from connections

- Greater reach with all of your information
- Able to connect others (and yourself) to distant contacts

Cons:

- Looking like a unstructured networker
- Can lead to lots of spam and sales messages
- Lots of information to sift through
- Harder to manage contacts
- May look confusing to those with very targeted connections

Can you start to see why I sit on the fence on this one? Most people have a clear idea on what they are comfortable with or what their preference is. It is far easier to start with the first camp and then move to the second camp if you prefer.

When we run training on LinkedIn or work with individuals, many users swing from one camp to the other. As they discover more about LinkedIn they clarify what they want from it, how they will use it and how much time they will dedicate to growing their online connections.

Once you have decided how you wish to manage your account and what approach you would like to take, then use our well developed and sophisticated method to identify all of those contacts you should connect with. It's that two step process we discussed in Chapter 1, but here's a quick reminder: a pen or pencil and a sheet of paper then the next part depends on whether this is being done at work or at home. The magic ingredient is a good coffee a strong tea, or if you are home, a nice glass of wine or whatever your favourite tipple is. Then start a list of everyone you should connect with.

Here are some areas you might want to explore and list:

- Business contacts
- Customers
- Suppliers

- Contacts you have from face to face networking
- People in your building or office
- Who you know in a business environment
- Your personal contacts (see your phone address book)
- Anyone you worked with in the past
- Previous customers or suppliers
- Friends and family (do we know what they do and do they know what we do? That's a whole other book right there!)
- Social contacts
- Old college or university contacts
- Neighbours

TOP TIP – you might need more than one sheet of paper! There are lots of other areas to consider, but as you start this process you will find a whole host of people to connect with.

Once you have your list it's a simple process of deciding who on the list you want to connect up with. There may be some contacts on your list, that for whatever reason, you don't want to connect with and that's fine - you don't need to send them a request. You may have some tenuous contacts (those you really aren't sure about) and depending on which camp you are in, this might be a simple choice. If you want to connect with as many people as possible, then I would suggest you connect up. If you are being selective, then review these marginal contacts and ask yourself – "why should I connect to this person?" or "What are the reasons for not connecting up with this person?" A little time invested can help you clearly decide.

It's worth reminding that LinkedIn provides some excellent easy to use tools that connect with all of your contacts in your email and other accounts. These tools can send out connection requests en masse. But like many things in life, just because it's easier doesn't mean it is effective. A series of personalised invites delivered over a few weeks is much more effective than a standard message. Clearly the personalised invites will take a little longer, but in our experience the connection rate is significantly higher.

So it's a simple process of getting onto LinkedIn and sending an invite to each of these identified contacts. I would suggest you do this over a period of a few weeks (depending on the numbers). This will allow you time to personalise messages and spread out the impact of your network, who will get to see lots of connections to you and your account.

TOP TIP – each time you connect up with a new contact, it will show up in the main timeline of all of your existing contacts and in the contact list of the person you have just connected to. This can be a great way of showing activity and raising your profile on LinkedIn.

While we are on the subject of connections, the best advice I can give you for sending connection requests is to personalise them. Make them specific and explain why you want to connect. This makes the recipient far more likely to accept the request than they would if they just received a bland "I would like to add you to my LinkedIn connections". We know this from feedback from people we have worked with and the many discussions in LinkedIn groups as well. Thinking back to face to face networking, you would need to be specific to gain someone's interest for a follow up meeting, call or maintaining a relationship (in the business sense) and it is just the same when on LinkedIn. Take some time, be specific and make sure that you give a good reason for connecting up. This builds credibility in you as an individual and helps move you towards your goal (the more connection requests you send that get accepted the better).

How do I grow my contacts?

So far we have dealt with the direct approach of sending out connection requests to those contacts you already know. Now let's have a look at some of the processes that can be used to grow your online contacts. We are going to consider five different areas that can help you grow your network:

1. Raising your profile, being "active" on LinkedIn
2. Being found through your own key words in your profile
3. Using groups to find new contacts
4. Looking at others contacts
5. Pulling in contacts with great content and information

A simple barometer for all of this activity is by using the "Who's Viewed Your Profile" section (to get to this, hover over the Profile button on the LinkedIn homepage and a new menu "Who's Viewed Your Profile" appears or on the right of your home page). You can click on this to take you to the detailed information.

Who's Viewed Your Profile

15 Your profile has been viewed by 15 people in the past 3 days

▲**2** Your rank for profile views improved by 2% in the past 7 days

Unlock the full list with LinkedIn Premium

It will show who has been searching you out and those that have taken the time to have a look at what you do. I love seeing lots of people who look me up on LinkedIn following an event or meeting or some online activity. The latest version of "Who's Viewed Your Profile" gives detailed stats and information on the types of people looking at your profile along with where they work, what industry they are from and how they found your profile. This tool is a great one to look at how your activity is having an impact on LinkedIn. It is worth spending some time playing about with this part of your profile.

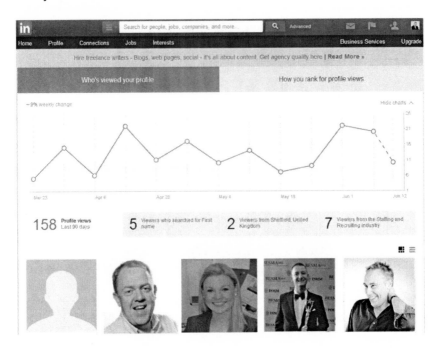

The more connections you make the more you start to identify. One connection often leads to several others. Once you are connecting with people from your original list, you will spot others on LinkedIn that you missed on your initial paper list (this often depends on the strength of the wine or favourite tipple). LinkedIn will frequently list "People You May Know" based on the connections you have. It is worth looking through these lists as they often have connections that you may have missed or not thought of. Think of this as ongoing work on LinkedIn, constantly topping up the connections that you have.

All of this work is about you actively finding and connecting with others. I would like to flip that over now and look at some of the ways you can attract people towards you, with the ultimate goal that they will be sending you connection requests. This is the face to face equivalent of the interesting and engaging person that others want to speak to at events or meetings. People gravitate towards them naturally to hear what they have to say.

1 Raising your profile, being "active" on LinkedIn

There is no clever marketing or sales approach here. These are the fundamentals of investing time on good LinkedIn housekeeping and keeping things up to date. You will find some top tips in later chapters that will help you, but the basics are here:

- Keep your profile up to date, current and relevant
- Accept requests to connect in a timely fashion
- Respond to messages in appropriate timescales
- Keep contacts up to date
- Share information (lots on this later)
- Comment, engage, share and talk (there's no point just observing – you will find life will pass you by)
- Log into LinkedIn regularly and get involved!

All of this activity raises your profile with your contacts (and other contacts depending on what you do). This can help people find you and connect with you. Think, if someone sees you commenting on a discussion and then looks at your (fabulous) profile, they may well send you a connection request. It's like when you try growing your business by getting out into the local business community. They don't come and knock on your office door, you have to go out and find them. Just the same at an exhibition; if you sit behind a table on your stand (that is a pet hate of mine), most people will walk past. If you stand up and start chatting to people you will raise the level of engagement and awareness of you and what you do. In this example specific focussed activity (towards the goals you laid out) will generate returns for you. I always recommend investing time in your LinkedIn activity and here is a great example where that time invested needs to be spread out over a period. There is little point in setting up your profile and generating a huge amount of connections initially, then not returning regularly to follow this up. We often see people face to face or on LinkedIn put some initial time in and then sit back. You need to keep the momentum going. Invest a small amount of time each day for the first few weeks, then keep a regular appointment to log into LinkedIn and keep your profile up to date and keep the connections coming in.

2 Be found through your own key words in your profile

This is a simple process of spending a little time considering the following question: "How would I like potential customers or key contacts to FIND me?" This is down to your profile and how you set it up (unless you skipped chapter 2!). It also relies on search and advanced searches that anyone can use on LinkedIn. We will address how to use these search techniques to help you find potential customers and contact in Chapter 6, but this is about people being able to find you on LinkedIn.

So take some time and consider what you would like to be found for. What search terms are appropriate to your potential customers or contacts and what is it you do for customers? The trap here is just listing your job role or title (all of the detail on this are in Chapter 2). The more people who can find you using basic and advance searches, the more chance that people will connect up with you and grow your online contacts.

This is the equivalent of raising your profile and making sure others know you and what you do in your business community or marketplace. I often hear people saying "it's not what you know, it's who you know". That might be true, but I have always worked with "It's not what you know, it's who knows you" - a slightly different approach, but a very important one! You need to make sure you are engaged with your contacts both off and online. You want to be first in the queue when a potential customer thinks about engaging a supplier for the products or services you offer. This clearly applies to working face to face or on LinkedIn; you want to be first in their mind (for all the right reasons) so you get the first opportunity.

3 Use groups to find new contacts

We will discuss group activity more in Chapter 7, but this is just to make you think about how new contacts can come from groups. You can search group members and decide which to connect with (the direct approach). Or, by engaging in good, useful activity in groups, people will approach you to connect as a means of following up on postings, information shared or discussions commented on.

If you meet regularly at any sort of group (I am part of two professional speaking organisations and several networking groups) then you build relationships with a whole new range of people. It's proved to be very useful for me individually, our business and our clients. This is the approach that will work on LinkedIn groups as well. Get to know people, which people are using which groups, interact with them and they are much more likely to connect up with you. This engagement and interaction makes you more appealing and naturally more people want to connect with you.

4 Look at others' contacts

Once you start connecting up with your list of connections you created at the start of the chapter, you will have the opportunity to look at your new contacts own connections. Imagine you connect up with your old boss from a previous job. You can have a look at their contacts (note this depends on their privacy settings) to find others you have worked with, such as suppliers, partners and customer contacts. This is a simple way of mopping up those contacts you may have overlooked or forgotten. This can take some time, so we always suggest you start with those that are most relevant and have the biggest number of connections. Spend some time looking through the list, and as you find useful contacts, personalise your message and send out that killer connection request.

5 Pull in contacts with great content and information

This step reinforces the importance of creating yourself as the "thought leader" in your area of expertise and shows the importance of sharing good content and information. For those of you familiar with, or currently using inbound content marketing you will recognise the importance of this approach (for those of you not using this, it is worth finding out more about inbound content marketing). This is key in helping you grow contacts by drawing people in towards you with the quality of what you do and share on LinkedIn. Imagine how great it is when you find someone who shares information that is relevant, useful and helps you do your job. You are likely to want to connect up with that person to ensure that you don't miss anything that they are saying. By investing time in getting the very best quality and quantity of information out, you will get the return of people wanting to connect up with you.

Everything we have talked about in this chapter is about growing your online contacts on LinkedIn. This is vital to improving your impact on LinkedIn, online generally and in face to face scenarios. We know that well networked people can spot more opportunities, create more connections and find more business. No individual can act alone in today's busy, time poor business environment. Following these tips you will maximise your impact and effectiveness through a strong and effective network of contacts on LinkedIn. We have shown how you can have a direct approach (sending invites) and draw people into you through great activity on LinkedIn. You may find over time that your focus will shift from the former to the latter, and like any piece of work, the more effort you put in the more you will get in return.

Remember that this isn't a one off activity. Looking at your connections on a regular basis, adding in new contacts as you meet them face to face and attracting people in with great content is an ongoing piece of work.

I look forward to receiving you personalised connection request!

CHAPTER 4

Securing recommendations

As part of growing a successful business we believe you need to focus on delivering great products and services to delight your customers. As part of this you will build a group of customers who come to love what you do. We call these advocates of your business. Advocates will tell others how great you are and help you secure new customers.

This is based on the sales cycle model below:

In this model, the suspect is someone who MIGHT need your product or service. There is no relationship, detailed knowledge or understanding of suspects yet, from your point of view (from their perspective, they probably don't even know you exist). As an example - if you sell business stationery then any business could be a suspect for you.

A prospect is one that you have engaged in some way and they haven't yet said "no"! The prospects are the ones that you have engaged in some way and have started to understand a little of what they do and how interested they might be in your offering. Continuing our stationary example, you meet 5 businesses at a networking event and 3 of them ask for your card and for you to send your stationery catalogue. What about the other two I hear you ask? Well one is another stationery company, therefore they wouldn't ever buy from you (they are one that will say "no" as they are in the same category as you). The other is supplied by a long standing business partner who they wouldn't move away from (they are second one that will say "no"). This is an important point to note that not all suspects become prospects. If they haven't said "no" at that initial contact then they move through to being prospects.

Once you have created a pool of prospects, businesses can start to win customers or clients (depending on your own preference or wording). We have a very specific definition of a customer or client. We define these as individuals who have purchased a product or service from you AND paid your bill. It's a small but very important point. Up until the moment when someone pays your bill, it's very hard to consider them as a customer or client. If in doubt, try to run your business for 6 months without sending bills out. Clearly it doesn't work as a long term business strategy. (**Note** – please don't try and run your business like this, we can tell you it doesn't work.) In our example we have two of the people we sent catalogues out to have now started ordering (and paying for!) their stationery from you.

The final part of the sales cycle is the advocate stage. These are the customers or clients who **love** what you do, they shout about what you do to other, new, prospects and help you grow your business. We need to nurture, develop and grow as many of these advocates as possible. In our stationery example, we do such a great job for one of the businesses they give us fantastic feedback about our service, delivery times and superior quality of the products we offer.

Many businesses have advocates of what they do, but they aren't quite sure what to do with them or how they can harness the power of advocacy. Here are a couple of ideas for you.

- Ask them to help you grow your business by helping to turn prospects and suspects into customers or clients. Sticking with our stationery example we could approach the advocate we created and say something like: "Frank, (assuming that's his name, if not insert the relevant name into this sentence) I know you have given us some great feedback about how well we have looked after you. Who else do you know who would benefit from our service?" It's with simple questions like this where we can get introductions to other potential customers. It is this sort of introduction that will help grow your business.
- The second way to harness the power of advocacy is to ask for a referral, either written or in video format (ideally both!). You can use these in a number of places and ways to show what your current customers are saying about you.

47

This can help you convert more suspects to prospects and more prospects to customers or clients.

> NOTE – This approach and connection is backed up by a number of groups, one in particular McKinsey & Company had this to say in their "The consumer decision journey paper."

"Our research found that two-thirds of the touch points during the active-evaluation phase involve consumer-driven marketing activities, such as Internet reviews and word-of-mouth recommendations from friends and family, as well as in-store interactions and recollections of past experiences."

So these are all great bits of very sound business advice, but how do they relate to using LinkedIn?

Well, everything we have described above (and lots more to come) applies on LinkedIn straight away.

Take the sales cycle; a large proportion of the contacts that you have could be classified into each of the four stages, suspects, prospects, clients and advocates (see notes later on about organising your contacts in Chapter 9). This will allow you to look at these groups and tailor your sales and marketing approach to each group.

In the context of this chapter the area we are focussing on is around your current customers or clients and the advocates that you currently have. We will be showing how you can leverage these relationships to find new contacts and potential customers.

Step 1 – This is simply looking at your current customers and advocates on LinkedIn, looking at their contacts, who do they know? Who are they connected to that you would like to speak to?

We use the MiNe model © to help ourselves and those we work with extend sales impact by focussing on the great sales and relationships that have been built up. This model was originally designed to be used as part of organisations general face to face sales process and the more we used it the more we realised that this is a simple and powerful tool to use on LinkedIn too.

First degree contacts	Second degree contacts	Third degree contacts
These are the clients you already deal with and who you know	These are additional people you don't yet know but who your first degree contacts also deal with	These are additional people you and your first degree contacts don't yet know but who your second degree contacts deal with
1. Get your sales message to these people – they understand what you can do for them in principle	Working with your first degree contacts, they act as your ambassadors, promoting you to the second degree contacts…	
2. Develop a relationship where you understand their needs and they understand that your solution will work for them		
3. They buy from you		
4. You have a strong relationship with a high degree of trust. Review opportunities to solve new issues with your solutions.	1. Get your sales message to these people – they understand what you can do for them in principle	
	2. Develop a relationship where you understand their needs and they understand that your solution will work for them	
	3. They buy from you	1. Get your sales message to these people – they understand what you can do for them in principle
	4. You have a strong relationship with a high degree of trust. Review opportunities to solve new issues with your solutions.	

This MiNe approach can be applied in a number of different ways, the MiNe name comes from the fact that you have to dig to find new connections and have to go through an in depth process and multiple layers of contacts to get to new connections.

LinkedIn provides an excellent tool to see how you are connected to the person you want to be in contact with. Once you have found the person, you can click on their profile on the right hand side there will be a section that looks like this:

How You're Connected

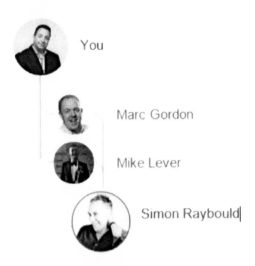

You

Marc Gordon

Mike Lever

Simon Raybould|

This might have several people that are connected to you that connect you to the person you want to connect with (Mike Lever in this example). The "Get introduced" clickable blue button allows you to write a short note so that Simon Raybould (in the picture shown) can pass onto Mike. Our recommendation is to use this only as a last resort.

This is a great example of mixing your online and offline approach to growing your network. Our suggestion is to pick up the phone and speak to Simon. You get a chance to understand how well Simon knows Mike and what their relationship is like. You might be able to find some more key information that will allow you to establish a better relationship with Mike. Once you have spoken to Simon you can ask him to speak to Mike and see if Mike would take a phone call from you or a meeting. You can then follow this up in the most appropriate way. A phone call or meeting is much more effective than a LinkedIn connection. Let's be clear the LinkedIn connection is still very important and will be a part of your preparation before your call or have the meeting. I very often send a LinkedIn connection request out that starts with something like "Following on from Simon's introduction and in advance of our meeting next week....."

These "warm" introductions are much more effective than a direct approach in either a face to face scenario or on LinkedIn. Imagine a person you don't know approaching you (on or offline) and them trying to engage with you and ultimately sell to you. It works but it can a slow and difficult process from both sides. Far better to have had a warm introduction from someone you know and trust that recommends a conversation with a third party you haven't yet met or know. This method raises the level of trust (see below for how important this is) and level of engagement. It shortens the process and makes it a simpler conversation from both perspectives.

Looking at business development and the most effective way of growing your networks, LinkedIn provides a great tool for introduction and we find that this approach (initially engaging offline, over the phone or face to face) is much more effective for the most important contacts.

It is also worth looking just below the link shown in the image above, if you scroll a little further down you will see this:

In Common with Mike

People Similar to Mike

This will potentially provide some additional background information about the individual you are wanting to connect with. It will show shared interests, areas, groups etc. This can be useful information when making that first contact or as part of a follow up meeting.

As you can see from the lower part of the picture above, LinkedIn also provides a potential list of other contacts similar to the profile you are currently viewing. It is worth looking though this to spot other great potential contacts you aren't yet connected with.

How else can you leverage the power of customers and advocates that you have on LinkedIn? The recommendations that these contacts can provide on LinkedIn can have a great effect on what you do and how you connect with others.

The power of TRUST

One of the most effective tools in understanding business growth is the power of trust. You may have come across the expression "people buy from people"; the full sentence is "people buy from people they know, like and trust". For the minute, we are going to focus on the trust part.

Charles H Green described this well and summarised this in a simple equation:

$$TRUST = \frac{Credibility + Reliability + Intimacy}{Self\text{-}orientation}$$

Consider each part of the equation when it comes to using LinkedIn:

Credibility is the part that comes when someone demonstrates their depth of knowledge, experience and range of experience in a given context. Credibility is shown through having all of the key information and being able to relay and use it in a positive way.

Reliability is the effect of keeping promises and "doing what you say you will do". It develops when someone's actions are congruent with the words that they use. Think about the feeling of frustration we have when someone promises to do a job for us then breaks that promise. Reliability can be based on experience and previous work.

Intimacy is the degree of closeness, relationship or connection we feel with another person. How safe and secure we feel with them.

Self-orientation is a description of the balance between focussing on themselves or focussing on you. It seeks to describe how aware the other person is of your needs and wants or whether they are focused on themselves. I often talk about this in the context of "living in your customer's world" and it has been described as "customer focussed" or "customer centric".

This tells us that that if we wish to increase trust (and I think most of us do) we need to focus on a few areas to tip the trust equation in our favour. Let's focus on what we can do on LinkedIn to raise the level of trust others have with us.

Credibility – a full and detailed profile with lots of information and background will start to establish credibility. Showing results, output or the effect of what you do builds your credibility. Giving clear examples of work and projects you have been involved with, or delivered yourself shows what you can do. Listing all of your qualifications, publications and projects can add depth to the level of credibility you demonstrate. Endorsements (see later chapters) should be a great way of showing credibility in that other endorse you in specific skills, however as we will see later, this may well not be the case.

Reliability – this can start to come from how you respond to questions and queries, how well you respond to discussions you have started and how you keep in contact with others. Reliability can also be reinforced from the contents of each recommendation on your profile. If others are saying how you helped them achieved their goals "on time" and "in budget" and "did exactly what they promised" you can see how this gives support to your reliability.

Intimacy and self-orientation are a little harder to demonstrate on LinkedIn. Here are a few ideas where you can start to show potential clients your approach. Help others, answer questions and point them to sources and contacts they might find useful. If you agree to contact someone, then do just that. Demonstrate how you are working with others through the way you describe yourself and the content you share in your profile. Think about the wording you use to describe the various parts of your profile, is it covered in "I" or does it involve a lot of "you" and "we"? The recommendations you get should reflect the fact that you are helping others achieve by focussing on delivering great results for them. This can really show that you are oriented more towards your customers rather than yourself. Thinking about your profile, both as whole and the individual sections: The focus on outcome for customers is critical, explaining how you help others and what you do for them demonstrates a real shift in self-orientation towards your customers or prospects.

The biggest influencer on all parts of the trust equation is through the power of the recommendations that you receive and show on LinkedIn. This is why taking a systematic, methodical approach to your recommendations will help you build trust and find new customers.

If we think about our own experiences as consumers, (either for ourselves, our businesses or organisations) we like to have a recommendation when we have no experience or knowledge in a particular marketplace. We ask others who they have used, who they recommend and who they would use again.

Using recommendations.

Let's examine how we go about building up recommendations that support this development of trust and we can start with a simple question.

What makes a great recommendation?

Ensuring you get the best quality recommendations on LinkedIn (and in your daily face to face work) is vitally important. Here are a few ideas to ensure that the recommendations on your profile are as powerful and effective as possible.

Think about who you ask for a recommendation. A more senior, well-known name giving you a recommendation will have more impact than a more junior team member. If you have been working with a Managing Director and her team, try to ensure that it is the MD herself who writes and posts the recommendation.

Have a clear objective about what your recommendations need to achieve. To help with this, think about the results you achieved with a customer, the effect you have had on their business and the short and long term benefits you have provided. Where possible, think about facts and figures to support and reinforce the overall picture.

TOP TIP - an effective way to think about a recommendation is that it paints a very small, short story of how effective you are. Look at the two examples below.

"Mike did a fantastic job for our company, his enthusiasm and knowledge was second to none. We would highly recommend Mike to others"

"Mike delivered 10 fantastic days of management training to the management teams in XYZ Manufacturing. His detailed knowledge and experience allowed him to tailor the course to our mangers' specific needs. He helped motivate and enthuse a team

of long term and experienced managers. Mike's own experience and hands-on approach brought the training to life and helped embed the learning in such a way that we saw immediate effects, as well as creating long term benefits we can see throughout the business. Everyone gave great feedback, but the real proof came when we saw that absenteeism had dropped by over 25%, project delivery against timescales improved by 15% and every manager completed their teams' one to one within an agreed timescale (something we had not been previously able to achieve). We have recommended Mike to other organisations and we will continue to do so."

The first recommendation looks fine, but, I am sure you agree, the second one looks much more powerful and paints a clear picture of what was achieved. It brings to life what was done and would make a reader want to know more. The second recommendation also indicates who Mike did the work for and is more specific about what was delivered. This reinforces the fact that recommendations can be used to build up trust with those looking to work with you. It helps potential customers look at what you do and approach you to do something similar with them!

So, you might be thinking, how do I go about getting a recommendation at all, but more than that how do I get a recommendation like the second example?

The first step is to ask. As simple as that; so many people don't take the time to ask customers to write a recommendation. Thinking back to the start of this chapter and the sales cycle, I have a very straight forward approach to follow up completing any part of work with a customer; I ask a handful of questions:

1. What other potential work are you looking at?
2. What other departments / groups / individuals should I speak to within their organisation?
3. Who else can they introduce me to (introductions to 2 other potential customers where possible)?

4. Finally, I ask for a recommendation. I ask for a written recommendation that can be used on LinkedIn, on our website and also ask for a video recommendation

The order of questions is important to me as this is the order that will get me the maximum possible business. Ideally, selling more of what we do to existing customers who already love what we do is the simplest, most effective and one of the most overlooked ways of getting more sales. The next is thinking about the other parts of the business that your product or service would apply to. The third is branching out and looking for completely new customers. The last step is about building a clear record of what you did along with the results that you can share with other prospects.

What happens if your customer doesn't have time to write a recommendation for you, or isn't good at expressing what you have done for them? You need to be prepared to help shape great recommendations. If a client really wants to help but is short of time, then you can draft a sample recommendation (remember you can't post this onto LinkedIn), ask your customer to amend and complete the recommendation and post it. This gentle nudge and support can help you secure additional recommendations. There are occasions when customers post a recommendation and it lacks the impact and insight that is important to you. LinkedIn allows you to request an amended recommendation and we often find having a conversation about this allows you to clarify the customer's thoughts and explain what you want. Don't be afraid to steer your customer towards the facts and figures above; they are often overlooked, but they provide the most effective recommendations.

There are a few other areas to consider with recommendations:

- Make sure you always think about giving recommendations first. Whenever we work with directors or teams, we always ask them to start the process by giving recommendations to those they work with first. This shows credibility and that you take LinkedIn as a serious part of your business work. (See note below on swapping recommendations though)

- Think about who you GIVE recommendations to. This is a reflection on you as an individual (think about the intimacy and self-orientation part of the trust equation). A well thought out recommendation demonstrates your professional approach. It can demonstrate your collaborative approach and the value you place on others.

- Be careful about "swapping" recommendations. I have seen a number of people on LinkedIn pass recommendations back and forward. Person A recommends person B and within a day Person B writes a recommendation for person A. I always feel (and many others have told me the same) that this seems to reduce (or remove) the impact of those recommendations. It's worth noting you can always choose not to display a swapped recommendation immediately.

- If someone writes a recommendation and it doesn't reflect you or your work, you can ask them to re-write it.

- You don't have to show every recommendation on your profile on LinkedIn. You can choose whether to show a recommendation. I have one or two that I choose not to show!

- Asking for recommendations should be a standard part of your sales process and follow up. Make sure that you have a follow up process once a sale is complete and as part of that, you are requesting recommendations for your website and on LinkedIn.

We have looked at the trust element from a LinkedIn perspective (this is a book about LinkedIn after all). If you reread this chapter or at least look at the key points you can see that all of these practices apply to your face to face, day to day work as well. The principals are sound, well thought out, tried and tested. All we have done is learn to apply these on LinkedIn to develop the very best level of trust with your suspects, prospects, customers and advocates as possible. This raised level of trust helps you connect with others, build more powerful and influential networks and ultimately sell more of your products and services.

CHAPTER 5

Finding your ideal customers and contacts

Whenever we ask an individual or a group what they want to use LinkedIn for, this is generally one of the most frequent responses: - LinkedIn is a fantastic people resource with over 300 + Million users worldwide. Chances are there will be at least some people on there you might want to speak to!

Let's start by considering who we want to speak to, or more specifically, who would we like to work with that we don't currently. Many individuals and organisations we see haven't invested the time to think about and clarify who they are aiming to work with. The ideal is to have a very clear list of businesses (or groups of potential customers if you sell to consumers) to focus on. Depending on the size of your organisation or your aspirations, you might put together a list of 10 to 20 business prospects you would like to work with and sell to. As a starter for 10, make this list visible and known. Put the list up in your office to remind you each day and tell your colleagues and network of contacts. You will be surprised at the strength and depth of business and personal connections you have in the people around you. We have found that when we work with a team at a company and help them draw up their list of 10 – 20 prospects, someone in the room will say "I know Susan at XYX...." Or "I used to work with Phil at ABC..." Just the act of clarifying this list will help you move towards being connected to and doing work with these target organisations.

As an example, we were working with an organisation on sales development and we were talking through the MiNe model (see the note in chapter 4). We split the group into 4 teams and asked them to list the companies that they wanted to engage and work with. We then asked the group to present their lists individually so we could create one master list of suspects and prospects that they needed to engage to convert into customers. The first person to present back was the MD. She started to run through the list of companies that her group had identified. It was the third company in the list that raised the attention of one of the other group members (an employee who worked on reception). This lady interrupted the presentation by saying that her brother in law was a director at that particular organisation. The MD cursed a little, saying that she had been trying to get in contact with that organisation for over a year now. The lady from reception offered to pick up the phone there and then and set the appointment up. Once you have created your list, share it with all of your team(s), employees and trusted business contacts. It never ceases to amaze me how well connected people are if you take the time to stop and ask them!

NOTE – as part of this list, a lot of organisations have a headline prospect that they would really like to work with. You probably have an organisation that you thought about yourself in one of those "wouldn't it be great to...." moments. It is worthwhile listing these prospects, as even doing a small amount of business with one of these headline customers can help you win others.

TOP TIP – some organisations find it difficult to create a crystal clear list of target customers. If this is the case for you or your organisation, start to think about building a profile of the ideal client. You can use criteria like size of the organisation, number of employees, geographic location, industry sector or specific market they work in.

TOP TIP – once you start to find, connect and work with this list, keep topping up and refreshing your target list. If you start with 20 and win some of these, then keep topping up the list so you always have 20 target customers to go after.

If you have followed the approach in the last chapter then your first port of call should be all of the ideas we discuss there. Use the MiNe model to use existing connections to get you introduced; use your advocates to get you introduced where they are connected to your list of 20 prospects.

But what if no one you currently know is connected to any of the list of 20 prospects you have created? In this chapter we will share the following ideas and approaches:

- Understanding where your customers (and prospects) "hang out" online and offline
- Researching existing customers to help you find new prospects
- Looking into areas of interest
- Researching existing customers to build a profile of prospects described above

A lot of this work will be based around getting a deeper understanding of your existing clients and customers, so if you skipped chapter 4 and the part about connecting to existing customers it will be worth revisiting that section.

Where do you start with researching current customers?

NOTE – this is about looking at your best customers on LinkedIn, not your connections. Focus on those customers who have given you most business or profit (after all, I am sure you would like to have a few more of these).

We have created a simple form for you to use to gather the most relevant information.

This is included below:

Company Name	Individual Contact Name	Key Words	Location	Industry	Groups	Other

To start this process, all you need to do is look at a selection of your current customers' profiles on LinkedIn. Look at each individual profile and list all of the details against them in the form above.

The first two columns should be self-explanatory (if not, well done for making it this far into this book without eating it).

For Key Words: Look at the words that immediately follow on from a person's name on their LinkedIn profiles. Don't bother listing company names or job titles, look for all of the other words that individuals use to describe themselves. List as many words as possible.

The fourth column is a simple case of listing the location of each customer (this isn't always shown on their profile if they haven't filled it in themselves). Just below the key words there will be a description of where an individual is based. Simply list this against each customer.

In the Industry column (likewise some people haven't completed this on their profile so it may be missing), fill in the industry that each customer lists themselves against. Again this is controlled by the central bank of information that LinkedIn provides and you will find it below the key words and to the right of the location.

The sixth column is used to list all of the groups that existing customers are using. You will find that groups are listed near the bottom of their individual profiles.

TOP TIP – not everyone displays all of the groups they are part of on LinkedIn. They (and you) can choose not to display the logos of particular groups. See more details in group work in our next chapter.

The last column is used to capture and note anything else that may be useful or worthwhile. We have listed some examples of things you may want to consider noting:

- Companies they follow
- Colleges, Universities or schools they attended
- Professional qualifications they have
- Offline groups they attend
- Any projects they are working on
- Previous companies they worked at
- Other courses they have completed
- Interests or hobbies

This can take some time, but it is important to fill in as much information as possible to give you a good overall view of your existing customers.

The information you collect and use as part of this exercise will be used in this and in subsequent chapters, so it is worthwhile spending some time and gathering as much information and research as possible.

Using this information in searches.

The first way to use this information is to use LinkedIn's great *Search* and *Advanced Search* facilities. We will describe this in detail in Chapter 8. Using the techniques described in Chapter 8, you will be able to search for new prospects by using the information and key words you have identified from your existing customers. As an example, if a lot of your current customers use the key words "Financial Controller" then searching for these key words will help you find new potential contacts and customers.

Where do your customers hang out?

The second way to use this is around understanding where your customers "hang out". This breaks down into two main areas.

- What groups they use on LinkedIn. If your existing customers are all part of a couple of key groups, then you need to join those groups straight away. It's a fair assumption to make that if existing customers or clients are in a group, then some of your prospects could be in there too. We will describe in detail how to use groups effectively to engage customers and prospects in our next chapter.
- Understanding what offline or face to face meetings and / or groups that your customers attend. Look at what they list, both from a professional and personal perspective. Is there is a recurring pattern? If so, would it be worth

exploring if you can attend, present at, or get involved with these groups?

Both of these processes are simple and effective and based on the principal of "fishing where the fish are". There is little point in looking for prospects in groups (online or offline) if there are only likely to be a few prospects there. It's far better to invest your time (your most precious resource) where you are likely to get a much higher return for your effort.

The work you have done around researching existing clients will also help you profile new prospects. If you find yourself thinking about how you grow your business, then looking at this information will help you in building the profile we described at the start of this chapter.

Many organisations don't have a clear perspective on what a great or ideal client would look like. Doing this research around your existing customers or clients can help clarify this point. This relates back to goal setting; the very purpose of setting a goal (in this case a list of customers) is extremely useful. Building a plan and taking steps to move towards these goals (customers) is when things start to get very exciting.

CHAPTER 6

Using group work online

LinkedIn has such a variety of groups available for you to join. They provide an excellent resource for a range of activities and we would certainly recommend spending time looking into groups and how you can use them effectively. For us, group work breaks down into two key areas.

- Using groups for personal and professional development
- Using groups to grow contacts, identify suspects or prospects and win customers

It is useful at this point to understand how you can use groups and what functions they have. All of the areas that we discuss in the rest of this chapter will be helped by understanding the fundamentals of groups on LinkedIn. The two major types of groups on LinkedIn are the closed and open groups. The former, you request to join and one of the group administrators will review your application and either accept or decline your request to join. This is often done to ensure that the quality of group member is maintained and they aren't inviting members in who will spam, sell to or abuse the group system. The latter is a group you click to join and you are accepted and therefore become a group member immediately. Some of the groups you approach will be closed and it is worth noting that a lot of group administrators will look at your profile to see if you would be a suitable group member. All the more reason to have a fantastic looking, professional profile.

Once you join a group the five areas that you will see listed at the top of the group's page are:

Discussions   Promotions   Jobs   Members   Search

Starting with Discussions, this is the default setting as you look at a group. Scrolling down a page you can see all of the discussions that have been posted by group members. It's a good way to see how active a group is by looking at the number of recent conversations taking place. A quick glance at the number of conversations, how recent they are and how many people have commented on them will give a good indication of the activity level and engagement of all of the group members.

Promotions.

Promotions is an area that is generally used for the direct sales approach (although lots appear in discussions). You would use this area if you wanted to let people know about a book you had written, wanted to promote a new product or had a new offer.

Jobs

The Jobs section is worth exploring (even if you aren't looking for a job!). This area highlights organisations that are advertising vacancies via the group. It can be a useful source of information as to who could be expanding, an insight into how a company works and what sort of people they are seeking to recruit. All of this can be useful information to understand if you are trying to sell to the organisation.

It's worth noting that the total number of members of a group is shown at the top right hand side next to the "Member" (if you are already part of the group) or "Join" (If you haven't yet joined) button at the top right of the group page. The "Members" on the menu above will take you to a full list of group members. LinkedIn helps here by ranking all of the members in connection order, 1st, 2nd and then others. Again, take some time to browse through this list to get a feel for the group members, their industries or their backgrounds.

Search

The search function opens up a new menu that allows you to search for the detail within a group. You can search for specific discussions, polls, the manager's choice discussions and a whole range of other parts of group interactions.

LinkedIn also provides lot of background information on the group. If you look at the "i" button to the right of the "Member" or "Join" button it will tell you things like how long the group has been running, the group owner and some useful statistics around the profile of group members. It's worth having a look at this information when you are considering using or joining groups.

Let's start by looking at how you can use groups for your own development. I am not sure what industry you are in, but I am confident that whatever you do there will be groups of like -minded people on LinkedIn that you can join in with. If you work in a particularly obscure industry then you may have a limited choice, but there will be groups out there. As examples, if you work in accountancy there are 1022 groups with the word "accountancy" in them. If its technology there are over 47,000 groups. If its taxidermy there are just 6 (but there ARE 6).

Once you join these groups there are a number of things you can use them for:

1. Keeping up to date with current trends and changes in the industry
2. News information
3. Polls and discussions
4. Jobs (both looking for them and advertising yourself)

Groups that have an active community and lots of discussions will provide a great way of addressing point one. A great idea is to look for any professional or accredited body that runs a group on LinkedIn. We would always suggest this is the best place to start from. These groups can be useful when you act as an observer and sit and read the information, discussions and updates that appear in the group. These groups that contain your peers can be useful for asking questions of, running new ideas past, or getting feedback, thoughts or input from people in your industry or marketplace. Please remember that some of your competitors may be active in these groups, so be aware of this when you post information.

Occasionally you can spot opportunities to work with others in the group. Often there are opportunities to collaborate or support others and our experience shows that building up a group of trusted connections in your own industry is always a good thing.

TOP TIP – you can choose whether or not you display your membership of any group on your profile or not. Sometimes I want to be part of a group for personal development, but not necessarily show this to potential customers who look at my profile. You can click on the "i" button and select the "Your Settings" button. In the next menu you can choose to display the group logo on your profile or not. You can also change some of the basic group settings here like; how many emails you receive from this group (this is very useful as a number of people have been put off using groups by leaving their setting at "receive daily updates" which means their mailboxes are filled very quickly). Lastly the "Leave Group" button is on this menu, so if you find yourself part of a group you no longer wish to be in simply click the "Leave Group" button.

Let's now look at how we can use groups to help you grow and develop your business. Before we start on this I need to be clear about the fundamental part on selling your products and services on LinkedIn

1. DON'T SELL!
2. If in doubt see point 1

This might sound strange coming from someone who is passionate about selling and business development. Think about this in the face to face environment; virtually everyone has a horror story of the sales person who is pushy and talks at you rather than to you. They push their products and services and says thing like "Oh I know exactly what you want" when you haven't had a chance to say a word. This is just the same on LinkedIn. You can spot people who spend all of their time just shouting their sales message time and time again, on the individual updates, company updates and especially in groups. Imagine this at a face to face networking meeting. The doors of the room burst open and a salesperson strides in and starts shouting how great their products and services are and how everyone should buy them. This approach doesn't work face to face and has the same results on LinkedIn. It's worth noting that these are often the people who say that LinkedIn doesn't work for them. It just goes to prove it ain't what you do it's the way that you do it (and that's what gets results).

This is about business development so it's important that we use an approach that will engage potential customers and put them in a position where they want to buy from you. This may sound like a subtle difference, but it is extremely significant in terms of impact and results. Just think about that for a minute. Rather than sell to prospects, you are putting prospects in a position where they would like to do business with you and buy your products and services. Think back to the trust equation we described in chapter 4 and more specifically the part about self-orientation. The "pushy" seller is very self-orientated, "I have a...", "I can give you...", "I guarantee..." An individual or organisation has the opportunity to take the completely opposite approach, one that focusses on the customer and therefore changes the balance of the equation.

Let's get into the meat of this process.

Back in chapter 5 we found a number of groups that your current customers use and we want to explore those groups to see if there may be prospects in there that we want to work with.

Once we have joined or been accepted (for closed groups) to a group, there is a simple process to follow.

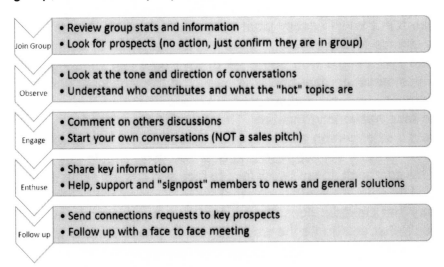

This is the process that we use ourselves, encourage our customers to use and recommend that you use.

This process does involve engaging the group, it needs you to interact with the group and ultimately end up in a position where you can follow up with a specific connection request. To reiterate one of the fundamental parts of this chapter, it is not about selling. If you approach a group in the way described above, you are building relationships, trust and knowledge. The group will understand who you are and what you do without the direct sales approach. Prospects react to this very well.

Using this attitude and approach is a great step towards "thought leadership", the process that highlights you as the "go to" person in your industry. This principal is based on you sharing, engaging and helping others with useful, relevant information. It involves engaging with suspects, prospects and customers outside of the traditional sales process. The model we describe above also supports the principals of "touch points". These touch points are the simple interactions with a suspect, prospect and customer that build awareness of you and your company. This process gives little gentle nudges to others and raises your profile. These touch points are an essential part of the selling process; Think back to the "people buy from people they know, like and trust" analogy; interacting with prospects and customers on LinkedIn is an excellent way of demonstrating trust and allowing others to get to know you.

Engaging in discussions

Let's look at the principals of getting involved in discussions in a group. It is important to start to engage with other conversations initially. Think back to face to face; everyone is in a room having lots of discussions and someone new comes in and starts a whole new conversation before engaging with anyone else. We need to be aware of a few simple principals that work well when using LinkedIn groups (note how much of this applies to your face to face work as well):

- Avoid taking over the conversation. At first engage and allow others to have their say and reply to ideas and information
- It's not a good idea to promote your products or services as part of conversation (it feels like pushy sales when you do this)
- Point out useful information sources, blogs and newsfeeds that help discussions
- Remember not everyone gets immediate notification of your conversation updates (some only get weekly updates) so don't always expect immediate responses
- Disagreement is fine, but avoid slanging matches (you would be surprised how often this happens)

By engaging in this two-way process (forgive me but some people need a gentle reminder that discussions are a two way process) you start to build up relationships and trust with others in that group. It's like meeting someone; you need to get to know them to decide whether you like and trust them. Participating in great two way dialogues and sharing some useful information is a great way of letting others get to know you.

There are a number of other areas to think about or use when it comes to groups.

Promotions: – Group owners can move items that aren't discussions to the promotions page. This allows you to look at what (and how) others are offering their products and services. You can follow particular promotions. For example, if you see a networking group being promoted you could follow the promotion and see how interactive the discussion is and how good and effective the event might be.

Jobs: – Firstly, review the number of jobs being advertised in the group. Simply click on the jobs link and see how many jobs are being advertised and how up to date they are. You can then create a job posting. If you share a group as an individual, then it will appear in all of the groups you are a member of. If you share a job from someone else it will do the same and appear in all of your groups. Group owners can advertise jobs directly in groups they control.

The final area to consider when it comes to groups is starting your own. This can be useful if your industry doesn't support or represent itself well on LinkedIn. You may want to start a regionally based group to interact with others in a way they currently don't on LinkedIn. Starting your own group can be really effective when there is a niche or an area that you think needs more representation. You can invite others on LinkedIn to join and you can promote your group as part of your day to day sales and marketing activity. You need to ensure that you get a good number of people to join the group and keep the level of interaction high within the group. This means you need to have regular content to share and information to post to the group. You need to work at this to encourage people to join and to start interacting and sharing information themselves. This creates momentum in the group, that in time allows you to step back a little and let the group start to grow and develop itself.

In summary, groups are a highly effective tool to use on LinkedIn. You can engage prospects and customers in groups. By not selling, you can start to build great connections, grow your contacts and develop the level of trust others have in you. Take some time to look at the groups that will help you achieve your goals. Look for groups that will help you with your own personal and professional development, where you can get up to date industry specific information. Finally look at groups where your prospects and customers are, get involved with these groups – fish where the fish are (no permits required!)

CHAPTER 7

Searching to find the right connections

The one area where LinkedIn's functionality is way in front of what you can do in your face to face work is the LinkedIn search function which is an excellent tool that will help you find those potential prospects and contacts that you are looking for on LinkedIn. If someone can find a way of replicating this in the face to face world - let me know, as that would indeed be a great tool!

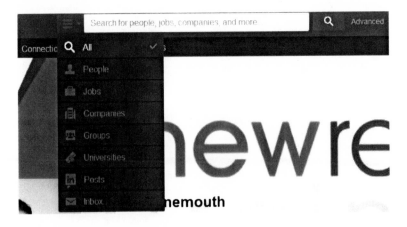

There are two types of search we are going to use and describe, advanced search and basic search. The basic search function appears at the top of the page on LinkedIn. Here you can simply type a person's name, company, group or keyword and LinkedIn will provide an excellent range of results. One thing to remember is that the default setting for the basic search tool is "All" (as in it will show results across people, companies, group etc.). It is possible to narrow your simple search by selecting a filter, for example if you click on the box just to the left of the search bar you are able to stipulate a search criteria (see the picture above). The list you can select from is:

- All (default)
- People: – this will show connections in order, i.e. 1st degree then 2nd degree connections. This search will return 1st, 2nd, 3rd degree as well as group contacts
- Jobs: – this allows you to search through all of the jobs currently posted on LinkedIn. Filters allow you to look at Relevance, Relationship, Date Posted (most recent), Date posted (earliest). As I write there are over 6000 jobs with the word Sales in the description
- Companies: – there are no filters on this search (see notes below) but if you search for general terms to find companies you will open up a huge amount of opportunities. As an example a search for "engineering" returns over 118,000 companies

- Groups: – simply type in a word you are interested in and find all of the groups you need. Journalism currently returns over 1000 groups results
- Universities: – simply type the name of your university or a university you like and find their information and a wealth of resources and contacts in their individual page
- Articles: – any current articles posted in news feeds
- Inbox: – contents of your own inbox, search for people or contents of any messages you have sent.

Just using the basic search function can get you a great deal of information and background. When you start to look for potential contacts or companies this is the place to start from. For example when you go to a networking meeting and bring back 5 business cards, simply type each individuals name into the search box and look at the returns. This is a great place to start as LinkedIn will show you how closely connected to a person you are. I like to be able to see who connects me and the person I have just met. This can be really useful when you want to expand your network as you can look at connections in common to see who else is a connected to the person that links you and the person on the new business card in front of you.

I have described the basic filters that LinkedIn gives you for each of the search criteria above. You will also notice that there are some further options on the left hand side of the page to help you refine your searches.

Company searches.

We searched for the term "Engineering" in the main search box under the Companies search. From this we got our list of over 118,000 companies. This might be a little much to work on at the minute, so let's see how we refine and focus our search. There are a number of simple things to get to the level of detail you need.

81

- Relationship – this section allows you to look at those organisations that employ people who are 1st and 2nd degree connections as well as providing a filter looks at 3rd degree and all other connections.
- Location – you can narrow search by country.
- Job opportunities – selecting this filter allows you to see organisations who are currently advertising jobs on LinkedIn.
- Industry – a deeper search that narrows your field of search by limiting results to one industry. To continue the engineering search, the industry terms LinkedIn brings up include "Civil Engineering", "Information Technology", "Mechanical or Industrial Engineering", "Construction" or "Staffing and Recruitment". You can also add another industry type by selecting the "Add" button and typing in your own term.
- Company size – LinkedIn offers a range of options that you simply select by tick boxes, anywhere from 1-10 up to 10,000 employees.
- Number of followers – this is the number of followers each company page has on LinkedIn.
- Fortune – this shows if any of the organisations are in any of the fortune listings. The range varies from Fortune 50 (largest) through to Fortune 501-1000.

This is extremely powerful information to use when you are using the basic search functions. Thinking back to the exercises in chapter 6, you identified some target organisations you wanted to follow up as potential prospects. You should already be able to see how the simple search function can help you identify, target and research all of those prospects. Using this search function allows you to narrow your search results to get to the specific customers you are looking for. Thinking about the engineering example above, you could look for larger (employs more people) civil engineering companies with lots of followers that are geographically close to you.

An alternative way to approach this is a simple exercise to 'reverse engineer' this work, search in broad terms and firstly see where your current clients appear in the search results. Look at the company size and see if this reflects their actual size (bear in mind others you are searching for might not have accurate information either). This exercise can help you clarify the filters you need to use to find new potential prospects. It's worth investing time in using the basic search and filters, as the information you can get out of this easy to use tool is well worth a small amount of time invested.

NOTE – with the basic version of LinkedIn (i.e. not a paid for version) you are only able to review the first 100 search returns on people, if you want to view more you must either change the way you search (narrow the focus), use advance search or upgrade to the paid for versions of LinkedIn.

Using advanced search

The second area to look at and use is the advanced search function that LinkedIn provides to all users. We have already seen that the basic search function can give you some excellent results, but the advanced search is a fantastic tool that can really help you find what you need. Not many people take the time to understand the advanced search functions and I would encourage you to spend some time playing about with this part of LinkedIn. It can help you take some shortcuts and find the prospects, people and connections you need quickly and easily.

Let's start by looking at the advanced search box. Click on the "advanced" word that appears to the right of the main search box at the top of the page on LinkedIn (see the image below). Note that the advanced search function is only available on "People" and "Jobs". I use this function regularly and find the people based search functions and details are fantastic. Think about this in terms of your face to face contacts and networks you have. LinkedIn allows you to explore and understand those you are directly connected to. It will show how you are connected to them and who they are connected to themselves. It gives you a clear insight to your extended network and helps by suggesting how you might get access to this extended network. The offline equivalent would be having access to all of your contacts' personal address books or list of names in their phone books. Imagine if you had that power, to flick though others contacts and then say "Hey can you help me speak to these people you know?" That is exactly what we are going to use the advanced search function for.

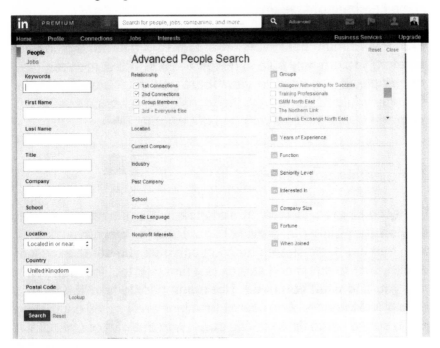

Let's now look at the details that advanced search brings up. To keep this simple I am going to describe the "People" advanced search as a lot of the information is mirrored in the "Jobs" advanced search.

The advanced search will bring up a new window in LinkedIn (as shown above). We will start from the options on the left of this new window and work our way across.

The options on the left are as follows:

Keywords – you might search for a specific term such as sales, advertising, aerospace or HTML.

First name – yes you guessed it, for searches when you only have a first name.

Last name – in complete contrast to above this is for searching when you only have a surname.

Title – this is the job function part, i.e. director, MD, owner or manager.

Company – when you have a company name and want to search through all of a company's employees.

School – the school that people attended (if they have completed this).

Location – this is a drop down box that allows you to specify anywhere (make the next options disappear) or to narrow your search by giving geographical criteria.

Country – if you have selected "anywhere" in the location options then this will disappear. You can choose from the list of countries that LinkedIn provides.

Postal Code or ZIP code if you are based in America – this allows you to type a postal code and as you do, LinkedIn will bring up an additional box that will allow you to select a radius to run a search on. This ranges from 10 miles (15 of those new-fangled kilometres) to 100 miles (160km).

You can immediately see (I hope) that this information is simply fantastic. The depth and range of options available to you open a whole new range of possibilities when using LinkedIn.

Before we look at the rest of the advanced search criteria let's have a look at some of the ways we can use these options to find what we need. The most common ways I tend to use advanced search is simply by using the keyword and typing a specific term and then using the geographical search to narrow the returns.

As an example, I am looking for Aerospace engineers in two specific areas, in the "Keywords" box I type that specific term, aerospace engineer (note I dropped the "s" as most people don't describe themselves in the plural). The "s", when left in or removed provides dramatically different results. Taking the "s" off returns over 450,000 results and with the "s" we get just over 11,000 results. You need to ensure that the keywords that you search are the ones that people will use in their profiles otherwise it will skew your results.

Now, I said I was looking for two specific areas. The first I want to look at, is within 10 miles of Newcastle Upon Tyne (United Kingdom) so I simply type in NE1 (Newcastle Upon Tyne city centre postcode) into the relevant search box on the left of the advanced search, then select the "10 Miles" from the dropdown list of "within" that appears as I type the postcode in. This search returns 280 results and this is a nice narrow field to start to look into details. If I repeat this search for my other location of Chicago and use a zip code of 60601, I get 856 results. In this example I have created a list of over 1000 people in the two areas I was looking for (just a 10 mile radius of two very small and specific areas). Try this yourself; pick some very specific keywords and the narrowest geographic search (try your local area first) and you will see how many local contacts there are.

This is where we really start to bring the exercise in Chapter 6 to life. If your existing customers are local organisations that employ a financial director, then all you need to do is search the term "financial director" in the key words search box and suggest a region across which you want to look for prospects. Sat in Durham (UK) this morning, running that search on "financial director" I can find over 5,300 search results for people within a

50 mile radius of where I am sitting. This gives me a great suspect list to start with. We have already explored how you go about connecting with people (in terms of building a relationship and connecting with them on LinkedIn).

These examples show just how powerful this advanced search is. In both of the simple examples above we have generated a list of suspects with a few simple clicks. Depending on how closely connected to these individuals you are and what version of LinkedIn you use (paid or not) will determine the level of detail you can see immediately on these suspects.

Now if we wanted to, we can refine that search even further, by using the other options that LinkedIn provides in the advanced search function. The first column to the left allows you to filter by looking into more of the detail in the following ways:

- Relationship – you can select any of the options below to see how closely you are connected to your search results.
    - 1st connections
    - 2nd connections
    - Group members
    - 3rd & everyone else

- Location - allows you to add a specific location for your search.
- Current company – specify a company that the person is currently showing as working at in their profile.
- Industry – select the industry you want to look into (this creates a drop down list and tick boxes. If you want to target specific industries this is a great tool).
- Past company – select a company that they might show on their profile as having worked at previously.
- School – school they attended.
- Profile language – look for contacts who have their profile in another language.

Just by using some of these parameters we are able to create a really focussed and targeted search that will get you the specific results you are looking for.

Using search criteria

The final list of search criteria appears on the far right of the advanced search options. Let's look at how we can use these. (Note that a lot of these options are only available to premium account holders)

- Groups – use the groups you are already in to narrow search criteria. With some group sizes of over 1.5 million members, using other criteria will help you sort through and find the connections you are looking for.
- Years of experience – this allows you to look at individuals with a specific amount of experience.
- Function – this option presents you a number of functional jobs in an organisation and you can select a number to help you refine the search details.
- Seniority level – this option narrows the search based on the seniority of your results. It is worth noting that you can search for particular job titles by using the keyword search.
- Interested in – this can be used to find people who have selected some specific criteria on their profile from "Potential employees" through to "deal-making contacts"
- Company size – this duplicates the company size filter already discussed in the main advanced search options.
- Fortune – choose the size of organisation by their position in the Fortune listing
- When joined – this can be used to find those who have just joined LinkedIn with options ranging from 1 day to 1-3 months ago.

All of these options are worth trying (if you have a premium account for the last few) to see how they have an impact on your results. Thinking back to the sales cycle (see reminder below)

The temptation might be to get as many suspects as possible (on the basis that the number of prospects is lower than suspects, the number of customers or clients is lower than the number of prospects). But a very specific list of suspects can reduce the drop out rate (and workload) moving suspects to prospects. Focus on what is important to you. If you have a volume business and need lots of customers then start with lots of suspects (qualified as best you can) and if you want a small number of customers then put the effort in to identifying the most effective list of suspects possible. The more work you do at the front end of filtering and clarifying will give you better results more aligned with your own criteria.

All of the work we have done on search boils down to you investing time in using the standard and advanced search to get you a list of suspects and prospects that will help grow your business. This is one of the most powerful business tools I know and time invested in getting to know and using this process regularly will help you grow your business.

What else do you need to know about search?

When you do find a person of interest, it is always worth looking at the function on the right of their profile headed up "People Also Viewed". This can be a hidden gem on LinkedIn if you haven't used it before. It gives you a list of other potential profiles (contacts) that might be worth taking a look at.

TOP TIP - list on a sheet of paper all of the names you see. The reason you do this is, as soon as you click on one of these you will inevitably look at the same section on their profile and click on another profile (and so on) until you find yourself 10 degrees away from where you started. All useful stuff, but make some notes along the way so you don't miss a potentially important profile.

People Also Viewed

Mike Lever
Current British Sales Trainer of the Year. Management Development & Sales Training, Coaching and Business Strategy

Chris Edmondson - Communications Maven
Communications Specialist at Base2

Marc Gordon
Connector of people, do you want more connections in your network?

Lyndsey Stephenson
Mortgage and Protection Adviser at Giraffe Financial - helping you make the right financial choices

A simple way to search is also to look at the "Who viewed my profile" on your own profile page. This is useful for keeping track of those who have taken time to look at your profile and it is often worth looking into their profile, look through their contacts and groups to see if they would be a useful contact. Very often if I find someone who has viewed my profile but not connected. I will drop them a connection request (personalised, obviously, quite often referencing the fact that they viewed my profile). This often sparks at least a dialogue online that can lead to a new connection or an opportunity to do some work.

TOP TIP – you can change the way LinkedIn presents information about you looking at others profiles (i.e. how you appear when they click on their version of "who has viewed my profile"). You can go into your setting (specifically "Privacy and Settings"), then look at "select what others see when you've viewed their profile" and choose from 3 options:

- Your name headline (LinkedIn recommends this). I use this one myself, I have no issue in letting others know I am looking at their profile
- Anonymous profile characteristics such as industry and title (I like to call this the LinkedIn lottery). When you click through an example like this, it gives a list of people who may have looked at your profile. You can often work this out, with someone you have recently met, called or emailed.
- You will be totally anonymous. This just lets people know that someone has looked at your profile, but gives no more detail.

NOTE – if you select either of the bottom two options then you will disable all of the stats you get about people looking at your profile and you will likewise not be able to see who has looked at your profile. For me, the first option remains the best. I do know some people will take a few days and use option 3 and look around all of their competitors on LinkedIn without giving anything away.

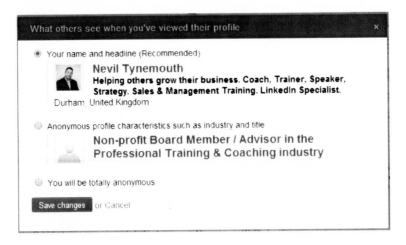

In short, the search functions that LinkedIn gives you are some of the most powerful business tools you can get access to. Using these tools regularly and employing the techniques described above will help you get to your goals. You can quickly and easily find new potential contacts and suspects to help you grow your business. Remember there are 300 million plus people on LinkedIn so there is sure to be a group of contacts on there that will be useful for you.

Chapter 8

Building your company page

⫯⫯⫯

LinkedIn is all about the personal profile and up until recently, the only other option for interaction was using groups. Now LinkedIn offers you the option of creating your very own company page. This is a great marketing tool that has many direct and indirect benefits and in this chapter we will look at how you build and maintain your company page and what you can use it for. We will also give you some guidelines about the pitfalls to avoid and best practice in engaging prospects, customers and contacts.

As we have tried to do throughout this book, let's try to relate this to face to face networking. You will want to engage and build relationships with the people you meet (remembering that people buy from people they know, like and trust). But you might be the face of a large organisation so you need to have a reference point that explains a little more about your company. This could be a brochure, a website or a video that gives more information about the company. The LinkedIn company page can help your contacts to find all of these things.

As part of this chapter describing company pages, we will also outline how you can use other peoples' company pages to find important information about potential prospects or contacts. There is a huge amount of information on LinkedIn (and it grows daily) and company pages are one area where the quality and volume of data is increasing constantly.

We recommend that everyone should have an up to date, engaging and friendly company page on LinkedIn. For the small amount of time it takes to build and maintain, it is well worth putting in when you realise the great rewards it can yield. The only time you might not consider a company page is if you are a freelance consultant (you are the business) or a sole trader or a one man band where clients associate with your name rather than the business. This is a small point, but an important one. We work with a range of companies in terms of their size and when it comes to email, some I file in my email using the company name and others I create files under the individual name. This is how I perceive my relationship with them and this is how I would perceive them on LinkedIn.

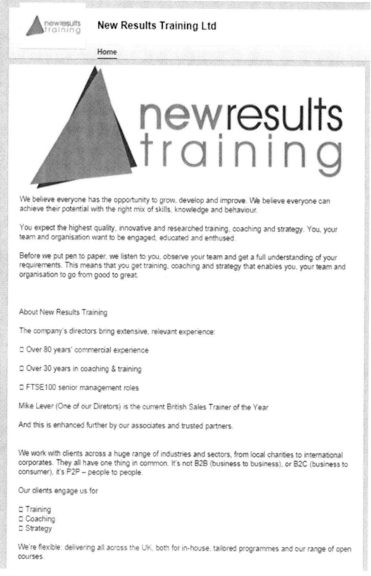

New Results Trainings company page. Find us and click follow!

Let's run through the basics of setting up your company page. Firstly remember that the LinkedIn help centre provides some excellent up to date videos on how to do things like this, so if in doubt, have a look at the Help Centre.

A company page is set up by creating a company page; this is NOT an individual profile with your company name on there (I still see examples of people doing this). LinkedIn will close down profiles that are created for a company and not an individual.

Getting started is really simple. Hover over the interests (little box) to the right of your name and as the menu drops down, look for "Companies" then click on the option to "Create". You will need to confirm your email address and full company name.

NOTE – you must have you personal profile set up in your full true name, otherwise LinkedIn will restrict you from building a company page.

If someone else has created a company page in your company name (you would be surprised how many times this happens and someone leaves the company) you will need to contact the LinkedIn help centre to transfer the admin rights to you.

Once you have done this it's a simple process to complete and you will need the following information:

- A good quality logo to upload.
- A fantastic overview of your company and what you do for customers (you are limited to 2000 characters – keep it simple and to the point).
- A simple set of answers to questions about company size, formation date etc.
- A list of the products and services you want to put on your LinkedIn company page (if at all possible list everything you do). See notes below on "Showcase Pages".

A good starting point is your main company website, brochures or marketing material that you use. Your LinkedIn company page should mirror the rest of your marketing, not stand alone or look significantly different.

Once you have the basics in place as described above, we can look at how we make your company page an effective sales and marketing tool for you.

Make sure all of your employees are following your company page (note that people, employees or not, "follow" your company they don't "connect" with it like people on LinkedIn).

Once you have set your company page up, if anyone searches for your company name in the search bar your page will present itself as part of the list. It's a simple job then to get employees and others to click the follow button when they look at your page. The follow button appears on the top right of the screen. Once you are following a company page then you will see updates from the page in your home page timeline. You will receive updates and information and will receive notification of new articles posted to company pages that you are following.

How can employees use their own company pages?

So why get all of your employees following your own company page?

1. They can share information from the company page. Rather than relying on your employees finding their own high quality information and articles they can simply share some (not necessarily all) of the articles you publish on your company page.
2. Communication! Whether you are a large or small organisation we have seen this over and over again where the whole team isn't aware of work or marketing campaigns currently running. By linking this information and sharing it via your company page, all of your employees see all of the information you are sharing with customers and prospects.
3. They can use marketing information and share the products and services you offer from a central point. (There is nothing worse than a customer having more up to date information

than one of your employees, but we still sometimes see this).

4. Getting an active page with lots of employee engagement will help to draw prospects and customers to your company page.

Obviously it will help boost the number of followers that your company page has and everyone can see how many people currently follow your company.

We mentioned above that employees can share information from your company page and in fact, anyone can share this information. So you need to create an interesting, engaging and targeted stream of information that you share from your company page. We have already discussed the "thought leadership" approach and the importance of trust, but it comes into play here on your company page too.

There is no point in just sharing your own content, yes you should share your own content, but unless you have an individual or team churning out, blogs, articles, white papers and books you will run out of great content very quickly; all of these are great to share and mix this up with other sources of information. Perhaps you worked with trusted partners and have great suppliers? You can share their updates and information (and in return they can share yours). This approach helps cement relationships and create a great online network, just like you have a great offline network. You can also look to some of the other areas we have described to find sources of great information, places like:

- Regulatory or central bodies for your marketplace
- Key market players
- Independent bodies
- Government websites
- News channels
- Professional development groups and websites

How do you decide if you should post an article? Make sure it will be useful for your current customers or the prospects you are chasing. That's it, as simple as thinking will my customers and prospects want to read this? Will it be useful for them? Does this help them or make their life easier? If you are answering yes then it looks like a good thing to post. The obvious caveat is that if it comes from a direct competitor or could damage your company brand or market standing then you don't post that (I didn't need to say that did I?).

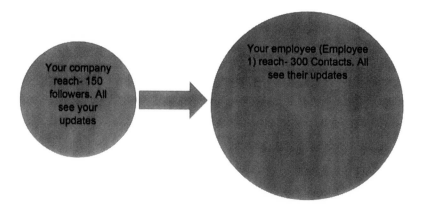

Now imagine you employ 8 people each with a minimum of 250 unique contacts:

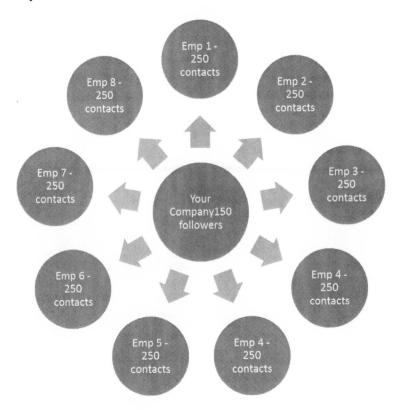

Assuming that there are 50 followers that none of your employees are connected to, one article or useful piece of information can be easily and quickly shared to 2050 unique contacts. That is a great reach for some of your key messages and communications.

Using Showcase pages.

You will also have the opportunity build "Showcase Pages" to list all of your products and services, but why take the time to do this? If you have some specific areas that you wish to highlight within your organisation, then showcase pages provide an excellent platform to do this. Be aware that people will need to "follow" each of your showcase pages (the maximum you can have is 10) as well as your company page. For many larger organisation this investment is well worthwhile as it will give a tailored, specific and relevant experience to each follower. For smaller organisations simply using the company page as the main focus works most effectively. Use either your company page or your showcase page facility to highlight what you do, how you do it and who you do it for. You can then draw customers and prospects into your company page and win some more business! You can create information steams and simply share this link out as part of the flow of information that you send out individually and from the company page or showcase page. Make sure you do a regular tidy up your products and services you list on both showcase and company pages, get them up to date and keep them up to date. Product specifications change, services get cancelled and new products get launched. Use the LinkedIn company and showcase pages just like a store front, get rid of the old stock and promote what's new!

You can choose to share any of this information mentioned above through peoples' timeline, out to groups or with specific individuals. Note here again, if all you share are links to your products and services, people will get bored very quickly and switch off from what you send. This is what traditional pushy sales does, just shout and provide a one way stream of information. Follow the thought leadership process and get lots of useful and engaging information out, along with the occasional sales message (no more than 10% - 20% of what you put out). This will keep people interested and keep them listening!

If you think of your digital or online footprint then the LinkedIn company and showcase pages should be an integral part that sits alongside all of the other social media platforms. With regard to your website; it is not an either or scenario, where you don't need one or the other; it is always best to have the biggest and most effective online footprint as possible. Think about the consistency as well; your website, other social media and LinkedIn company pages should have that consistent message, look and feel to them. This consistent marketing message and branding is something that marketing experts bang on about at length so I suppose we should listen to them (in this case).

The best LinkedIn company pages

Every year LinkedIn shares a list of the best company pages. It is always worth looking at these pages to see what you can learn from what they do, the current list of the best company pages include the following:

- Adobe
- Hubspot
- Kellogg's
- Four Seasons

When you review why these pages won the best company pages, there are a number of factors or reasons but the most important is the engagement level they have with followers. Whether it's through great content, rapid responses or innovative ways of engaging audiences, it's all about creating a company page that users want to follow. This makes the ideas above about content sharing and thought leadership even more important. It also supports the occasional sales message approach to an engaged and willing audience.

On the flipside, there are a number of company pages that are dead on arrival and more surprisingly, some of these are large organisations. We run exercises reviewing company pages and one of the things that stands out is how poor some company pages are. The company pages we have found to be the worst are .... No you didn't expect us to tell did you? Have a look yourself, look around your industry, your competitors and suppliers. List the things that they do well and avoid all of the points they have done badly, invest some time in your company page and it will give you the return.

To summarise this, think about how Walt Disney put it: *"Whatever you do, do it well. Do it so well that when people see you do it they will want to come back and see you do it again and they will want to bring others and show them how well you do what you do."*

If you engage followers effectively they will tell others and bring their friends!

CHAPTER 9

Getting organised and getting on!

Many people I speak to have dipped in and out of using LinkedIn or have had a few ideas and ways of working but chop and change their approach. Does this sound like you? In this chapter I will share a model that will help you focus on the most important areas to you.

First, where to start? You might have got so far in this book and thought, well all of this sounds great, but where do I need to focus and what time should I commit to this? This is probably the most common question I get asked. People get overwhelmed by the depth of a tool like LinkedIn and when they are unsure on what to do, they do what most of the human race does – they do something else; cup of tea, quick snack or a nice easy bit of filing. Let's make this easy and adopt a robust process you can use here and now.

20 minutes a day?

I call this my 20 minute a day plan, the simple day to day things that you need to do to really make the foundations work on LinkedIn. Let's look at the areas I am talking about:

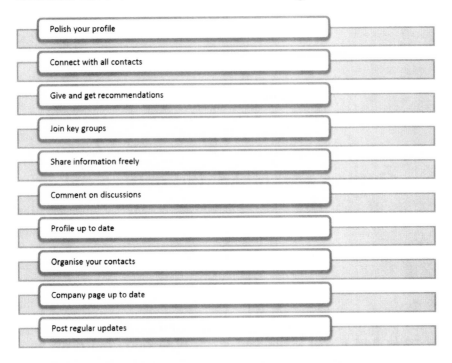

Polish your profile

Connect with all contacts

Give and get recommendations

Join key groups

Share information freely

Comment on discussions

Profile up to date

Organise your contacts

Company page up to date

Post regular updates

Now what I suggest is that you dedicate 20 minutes (we can all find 20 minutes if we try, can't we?) per day for the next three or four weeks to work on this list. Where you spend your 20 minutes depends on how well you are doing on LinkedIn so far. What we suggest is start from the top of the model and work your way down the list. Complete a review and mark yourself out of 10 in each of the areas. Be honest, what have you scored? Simply start with the areas that need most focus!

We have described in detail all of the major steps you need to take to work on these individual areas. To recap here would be just to create filler for this chapter and we don't do that.

Keeping on top of your growing contacts.

The one area not discussed anywhere else in the book and we will cover here, is the organisation of your contacts. This is quite a small point, but lots of people get very excited by this as it can really help you be more effective on LinkedIn. You can take control of your contacts and create simple groups that only you can see to help you keep track and target connections.

Let's look at how we do this:

If you look at all of your current connections (hover over the network tab and select contacts), LinkedIn is now providing you with more powerful tools to help you organise and engage with contacts.

You will be presented with a list of the people you have contacted most recently- Linked in highlights this with a little reminder that says "sort by **Recent Conversation**". Contacts you have messaged (via LinkedIn) recently will appear at the top of this list. It's a simple way of seeing those that you have engaged with recently. You can change this filter to three other options "sort by **Last Name**, **First Name** or **New**". It is worth noting that the last filter will show you all of the contacts you have connected with recently in order of most recent at the top. If you scroll down this list, you may see dates or number of days appear on the right hand side of some of your contacts, this denotes the last time you messaged a contact on LinkedIn.

Next to this is another drop down menu that is titled "Filter by". It is this one we want to look at it some detail. Before we get started on this let's have a look at a couple of key questions:

Do you use a CRM (Customer Relationship Management) system in your business?

Do you know who your friends are, who you know via networking groups, customers and prospects?

If the answer to either of the above questions is yes, then this chapter is particularly useful one for you. LinkedIn gives you the power to do just these things to help you keep on top of or maximise the relationships you have through contacts you have on LinkedIn. We are going to focus on the "Filter by" setting of "Tags". These are simple ways you can identify and group the contacts you have on LinkedIn. Now if you haven't used this before but run this filter you will find a list of your contacts already have tags associated with them. They will be things like "friends", "groups_members" or "colleagues". These tags are created automatically when someone connects with you on LinkedIn, for example if they (or you) sent a connection request that said you knew them through a group, then they will automatically be assigned the "groups_members" tag. This provides you a simple way of looking at people you have connected up to via your group work. You are equally able to find all of the people you work with currently or previously with the "colleagues" tag. Now all of this is ok, but where this becomes really powerful is when you start creating your own tags and applying these to your contacts. As an example you can create a tag of "prospects" and apply this tag to all of the contacts that you have that are prospective customers. This is how you do that:

- Hover over a single contact in your list.
- Three new icons will appear: "Tag", "Message" and "More".
- Click on the "Tag" icon.
- You will see a list of current tags (you can select if you wish).
- Or click "Add a new tags".
- A box will appear for you to create a new tag. Fill in the tag you want to create - in this example "Prospect".
- Click save.
- This contact will now have that tag associated with them.

For any other contacts, you won't need to create a new tag, simply click on the tag "prospect" you have created.

> NOTE you can also click on the "Manage tags" icon at the bottom of the tag menu and this will allow you to create and edit all of your tags from one menu.

You can create any number of tags that you would find useful, some ideas might be:

- Suspect
- Prospect
- Customer
- Advocate
- Lapsed customer
- Supplier
- Partner
- Group member
- Networking contact

Any contact can have multiple tags, so they can be a "customer", "partner" and "networking contact". Remember that your contacts can't see these tags, they are just for your own use on your LinkedIn profile.

Using tags effectively.

Once we have put this effort in, we need to work out how we can use all of this additional information. Firstly you can run a search in contact to look at all contacts who have a particular tag. Simply click on "Filter by All contacts" and then select "Tag" and click onto the tag you want to look for. This will bring up all contacts you have previously added this particular tag to. It is useful to have a look at that list on LinkedIn and keep track on what they are doing. I hope you are saying "So what?" at this point, because here is the brilliant bit, you can select a tag (let's stick with the "Prospect" tag you created) and it will bring up a list of results (assuming you have taken the time to tag each prospective customer with your "Prospect" tag. There will be a little box at the top of the list that says "Select all", clicking on this you get three new options:

- "Tag" allows you to add another tag if required
- "More"
- "Message" – this one is the key!

By using the message facility you can send a specific message to a specific group. Think about that for a moment, a particular message out to your prospects, your customers or colleagues. You can then take the same core message and personalise it to reflect the groups it goes out to. You will be able to quickly get the right information and messages out to the right groups. Simply write the message that you want to get out and then tailor it depending on the group receiving it. This tailored approach to your messages means that you can create more engagement and increase the chances of getting your messages read by the people who are most important to you. Imagine a quick way of getting a message out to networking contacts about a great new event you have heard about or some important information on an exhibition to your suppliers? This simple but powerful tool helps you create real targeted impact on LinkedIn.

Investing time on LinkedIn to get a return.

Invest a small amount of time (20 minutes per day) for a short period of time and you can achieve more than the vast majority of LinkedIn users. Invest a little more time in organising your contacts and really start to harness the power of LinkedIn.

The final bit of getting organised and getting on links to the first part of the book, thinking about why you as an individual are using LinkedIn. Are you doing all of the things you need to do to move towards your goals? Look at your activity regularly, depending on what you do on LinkedIn. Can you measure the return on the time invested? Track new prospects and opportunities that come to you as a result of using LinkedIn. Like any part of your working day, you should know what you are doing, the time you invest and returns it generates for you.

CHAPTER 10

Putting it into practice

This chapter is intended to act as a reminder or a check list of all the activities described so far in the book. You can use this as a short cut (to avoid reading all of the chapters) or as a reminder of key activity in each area.

Understanding why YOU use LinkedIn

- Have a clear idea on what you want to use LinkedIn for – write this goal down and refer back to it regularly. Is it for any of the following:
  - Sales and marketing plan.
  - Finding new customers or suppliers.
  - Keeping tabs on my competitors.
  - Increasing my knowledge and skills.
  - Keeping pace with my own market.
  - A content marketing tool.

- o   Raising your profile.
- o   Looking for a job.
- Create a list of contacts you would like to be connected to. Think about previous employers, colleagues, friends or family in business, suppliers etc.

Creating a brilliant LinkedIn profile

- This is the key area to get right. Invest more time here initially and keep updating and polishing your profile.
- Link this back to how you work in a face to face environment.
- Most important is getting a great business photo.
- Second most important is getting your key words right (those words that reflect what you do to help customers not, your company name and job title).
- Work through each stage of your profile and provide as much information as possible.
- Make sure all of your contact details are up to date and current and fill in as much detail here as possible.
- Embed videos and create links to your company (or other) website within your summary and job descriptions.
- Use the LinkedIn tools to review your profile and spot gaps in your profile. Answer all of the questions and fill your profile.

Building your online contacts and network

- Clarify why you are building your contacts and network.
- Decide whether to connect with everyone or be selective.
- Look at how you expand your network of contacts on LinkedIn.
- Send out personalised connection requests.
- Attract new contacts in by being active on LinkedIn.
- Review your "who has viewed my profile" tool to see how well you are engaging others.
- Use great key words to help others find you on LinkedIn.
- Connect with others through groups.
- Filter through others' contacts list.
- Pull in new contacts by sharing useful information.

Securing recommendations

- Refer to the sales cycle of suspects, prospects, customers / clients and advocates.
- Think about how you find new prospects or customers by working with advocates when you are face to face with them.
- Use the MiNe © model to identify new prospects via your existing customers and advocates.
- Use warm introductions from your advocates to get you in front of new prospects.
- Remember to think about how you build TRUST, the Charles H Green formula to influence what you do face to face and on LinkedIn.
- Think about what makes a great recommendation and help advocates write great recommendations for you. Be specific!
- Give recommendations first, show you are business focussed.
- Don't "swap" recommendations with others, this reduces the impact of what people say.
- Think about the other things advocates can do for you: more work with them or another part of their organisations, a direct introduction, a recommendation on LinkedIn or a video testimonial. Most people don't use the power of their advocates enough.

Finding your ideal customers and contacts

- Do you know what your ideal customer looks like?
- Have you built a specific list of customers you would like to work with?
- Understand who in your network might know these organisations (and individuals within them).
- Use your network to access these new prospects.
- Review your existing customers on LinkedIn and build a good overview to spot recurring patterns around:
  - Key words

- ○ Location
- ○ Industry
- ○ Groups

- Use this information to look for new prospects using LinkedIn's great search facilities.
- Learn to fish where the fish are!

Using group work online

- Groups fall into two categories: Those to raise your profile and find prospects and those that you can build your own knowledge and learning through.
- Explore groups fully to see how active they are, look at each aspect of a group before deciding to join.
- If you use groups to build knowledge, find the most dynamic groups in your industry and join them, participate fully and engage with others in the group.
- Using the research you completed into your existing customers look at the groups where more potential prospects might be and join them.
- Interact with a group – comment on existing conversations and add value with response and links to useful information (not sales material).
- Start your discussions and interact with the group (a great question can start a really good discussion).
- Number 1 rule is DON'T SELL, people don't respond to this in a group.
- Raise your profile, share information, solve problems and demonstrate to others you are a credible and useful contact.
- Use the processes of "thought leadership" and "inbound marketing". Both rely on you sharing useful and relevant information for your prospects and customers.

Searching to find the right connections

- LinkedIn's basic and advanced search both provide excellent tools to find prospects and new contacts.
- Using all of the information you have gathered about existing customers and use advanced search to find contacts in:
  - A specific geographical location
  - A particular industry
  - With key skills
  - With a given job title

- Using the search tool to see how your current customers are appearing on LinkedIn.
- Using the filters on the advanced search tool allowing you to narrow your search and find exactly the right contacts.
- Making use of existing contacts and customers to get warm introductions to new contacts and prospects.
- Checking who has viewed your profile using the tools on your home page.
- Adjusting your settings to decide whether you want to allow others to know that you have viewed their profile.

Building your company page

- Using a company page is a great way of generating activity.
- Deciding if a company page is right for you; if you are a sole trader it might not be.
- Building a page that attracts others in and makes them want to "follow" your page.
- Engaging those on your page with useful and new content.
- Making your page visually appealing will help new contacts and prospects stay the first time they land.
- Build "showcase pages" where you have significant part of the organisation you want to highlight out to prospects and customers.
- Finding key information to share via your company page.
- Matching up all of your other marketing activities with your company page is key.

- Getting all of your employees to share your company updates to their contacts
- Reviewing great company pages and your competitors' company pages for inspiration.

Getting organised and getting on

- Taking time to review your goals and activity on LinkedIn.
- Be honest with yourself. What could you improve on your personal profile or company page?
- Creating your 20 minute a day plan (to get started).
- Organising your contacts to useable groups.
- Planning how you will communicate with these groups.
- Invest time in getting all of your profile up to date. Equally invest time in engaging and interacting with others.

Appendix 1

The Art of LinkedIn

While doing the research for this book, I came up with lots of key information, ideas and processes that various organisations and individuals around the world are using. I looked at a number of blogs and heard lots of people talk about LinkedIn. There was an Art of using LinkedIn effectively that a number of people were pointing out.

This Art was none other than Art Flater. His profile came up regularly in our research. Art is the co-owner (with his business partner Chris Rosecky) of Central Office Systems and Central 3D Systems. Part of his role is to ensure top line revenue growth for the business. He does this by bringing new clients to the business while retaining revenue from existing clients. He has a "love it or hate it" profile: Some people really love it and some people don't like it at all. Take a look at it and decide for yourself.

For those of you away from an internet connection and can't see his profile immediately, let me paint you a picture. It's quirky, it's funny and it's unusual. Art looks at the lighter side of LinkedIn and the way he describes himself throughout the profile is just hugely entertaining; here are a few of the highlights:

- My ultimate goal is world domination of the military industrial complex, through control of 3D printed objects, printed documents, and electronically stored documents.
- Specialties: Exceptionally good with sarcastic, smart ass remarks.
- Invented the 2 hour lunch break, which has been adapted by sales slackers everywhere.
- I pretty much hang around and point out my staff's shortcomings, talk on the phone, and complain about how things should be.
- Talked on the phone and hung out. Took credit for others accomplishments.

I was lucky enough to interview Art for the book and get a really great insight in to his thoughts behind and reasons for his profile. To position this and Art's approach, it's worth sharing our initial contact:-

I dropped a fairly normal (but personalised) invitation to connect and asked Art about taking part in an interview for the book.

My invite:

Hi Art,

You have been referenced by a couple of people, I am writing a few articles on LinkedIn and I would like to connect up with you.

Any objections to mentioning you in an up and coming LinkedIn book?

Thanks

- Nevil

Art's response:

Nevil,

You can certainly use my name and profile in your book. If you would like to interview me or cover exactly what made me do this, I'm happy to help.

I have a couple of rules for connecting with me:

If I am ever in England, you are required to buy me drinks.

If I need someone roughed up or killed in England, you are my contact for that type of thing.

Oh, if you mention me in your book, you need to send me a copy.

Art

Apparently this is his standard reply when he is connecting with people outside of the USA (he later explained if some people didn't cough up the drinks he would invoke the roughed up clause from others to force them to buy him drinks – brilliant!).

So why did Art choose this approach? Some of the detail from our conversation sheds light on Art's rationale for his profile:

We discussed a great deal about his business generally and Art is a very switched on business owner. As we talked, Art shared the importance of sales and selling to business and an analogy about sales and business development. "In business as in sport (let's say cycling or running), everyone shares the lead or the lead group when you are on the flat even ground. Once you reach the hills that's when the lead changes and those with the real fortitude show their true colours." This is an analogy that Art shares with his team regularly.

Art clearly understands the business and importance of selling so why did he build such an unusual (anti?) profile?

According to Art "I was in a good mood when I started to fill in my profile" and LinkedIn kept asking me questions like "What did you do at your previous job?" so Art sat and thought, well what did I do? Hence the "went to lunch a lot" and "Pioneered the 2 hour lunch break". Art probably filled his profile in as many of us would like to, with a good dollop of humour and a reality check throughout.

Art has ended up with a profile that makes people smile and generates lots of interest in him and what he does.

The response Art got was, as you might expect, mixed. Some people loved it, others really don't like the light hearted approach that he has adopted. My own thoughts are that Art has got it just right. For him. He has a good mix of reality (as in what he really does) laced with great humour that engages people, this reflects his personality in business. This approach won't work for many others, but for Art, it is apt and appropriate. Anyone talking to him for a short period of time will see this.

Art talked about how his profile has generated interest. He says that you can tell when one person in an organisation finds his profile as he then gets a flurry of profile views within that same organisation. This is the power of networking with others, finding something good that they like and sharing it with their colleagues. He talks about the day he knew his profile had really hit the mark when he came back to the office to find 300+ emails with connection requests. He talks about little pockets of Art fans in Silicon Valley and on Wall Street. In short, Art has done what a lot of people are aspiring to do: raise their profile to lots of people they don't currently know.

Others didn't view his profile as a positive use of LinkedIn. Art describes one LinkedIn expert who thinks Art is "Dragging it (LinkedIn) through the mud and putting it in the pig's trough". Strong words, but Art knows and understands that not everyone will like his profile. The reason he knows this is that he understands that not everyone will like him face to face or want to do business with him. Art says he thinks there about 5 core personality types out there and he can work well with four out of these five. Hence the profile will work well with those people Art is trying to do business with, because the profile is a very good reflection of Art as a person. When we discussed the personality types, Art had this to say:

"The DISC profile breaks dominant personality traits in to 4 areas. It seems that there are lots of combinations based on the 4 major profile types. I kind of segment personalities in terms of 1-10 meek to aggressive

1-2 would be very timid 3-4 would be moderately timid 5-6 would be moderate 7-8 would be moderately aggressive and 9-10 would be aggressive

This is a simpler scale than the DISC scale, and easier to identify, but not as accurate. And at different times and looking at different subjects, personalities will adapt and change.

Depending on the subject and the individual, a sales person has to be able to adapt to the personalities as much as possible. It is difficult for a 9 or 10 to adapt to a 1 or 2, or vice versa."

As part of the discussions I was keen to understand what work or other benefits Art had as a result of his profile. His response? "I have, by accident". But not, perhaps in the way you would imagine. Because Art's profile has been seen by so many people and because so many of those people want to have a look at

Art's company, they click from LinkedIn and go to his company website. This has helped his Google ranking to the point where his company page has become the number one search return (after the paid for results) on Google in his industry. Being number one on Google is something that a lot of organisations strive for, so this has had some great knock on benefits for Art as Co-Owner. Also the huge number of connections that Art built up has helped raise his profile with a whole range of contacts on LinkedIn. On top of this Art has the benefit of his profile being seen and shared on a regular basis. This has allowed him to build up a huge range of connections that he previously might not have had access to, opening up new opportunities along the way.

One area that I have been involved with is around the psychology of consumer behaviour. A link appeared between what Art has done and our research and development for a new development programme. I worked on this with the rest of our team and Dr John Duggan (an expert psychologist). In our programme on the psychology of consumer behaviour we draw a link between happiness and decision making. The fact is, that those who are in a happy state are able to process more information so they are in a better position to make a decision in a buying situation. There isn't space to give you all of the insight here, but that one fact helps understand why Art's profile may work very well with a certain group of people.

The whole approach that Art has adopted on LinkedIn is very unusual and I was really keen to understand what Art had learned from this. His response was typical – "Ask my wife, she will tell you I haven't learned anything since we got married!" Once we got past that, the insights became a lot more, well insightful – "not everyone has to like me and that's their problem and not mine". "Life is too short for no sense of humour or not having fun". One of the most interesting insights was that "people don't look at your profile (but that is not a learning point)". Art explains he can tell those that have read his profile and those that haven't when they meet face to face. Those that have read the profile are waiting to meet, discuss and find out more about Art; it's almost like he has made himself interesting to others, attracting people in.

Art tells a very interesting story about a "sales chump" who approached Art to talk about his website and help to improve it. As part of this discussion the "chump" (what a great word by the way, so great I needed to type it twice and I might see if I can sneak it in a little later), mentioned social media, and Arts response? "Social Media, most of it is useless, no one on Facebook cares about printers and copiers, what a void in your life if you follow a printer and copier company on Facebook". Art continued to explain his views on Twitter "I am still not sure if Twitter works in a business to business environment. If I had a restaurant I would be all over Facebook and Twitter". The subject then came to LinkedIn and Art asked if the sales chump had looked at his profile, to which he got "yes I did" and as Art explained, "No, I am sure you haven't. If you had, you would be taking a very different approach to the meeting." Don't be a chump (and I am right with Art on this), if you are going to "sell" social media, be good at it and use it yourself. There is no other way to prove yourself to be credible. If you look at the Charles H Green trust equation in Chapter 4, this point becomes absolutely clear. If you want others to buy from you and trust you, you need to be great at what you do.

We then discussed what top tips Art could share on using LinkedIn:

- This approach won't work for everyone, in his words "My strategy might be risky for an employee". Bear in mind Art is the Co-Owner of Central Office Systems and as he points out himself "the chance of me hauling myself in the office and sacking myself is very slim".
- Get some of your personality into your profile (and realise that not everyone will like this).
- Make sure they don't dislike you (or to put it another way, make sure you do everything you can to draw people in and to like you, your profile and what you do)
- Get a good photo, nothing offensive and no holiday photos from a distance

Don't use the "stupid words", the business buzz words, keep it simple. When I asked which particular buzz words he didn't like – "Buzz words change too frequently for me to pick any favourites. I dislike hearing buzzwords as a substitute for real content."

Art also mentions some of the areas he avoids on LinkedIn:

- I don't connect with competitors – (some people do some people don't). The downside may be your competitors fishing through your contacts and looking at what you are doing.
- I don't connect with recruiters (I often get my profile viewed by recruiters looking for suitable candidates for roles they have to fill).
- Art also avoids the LiOn connections. These are the LinkedIn Open Networkers. They seek to get as many connections as possible, the number is the primary goal for them and he hasn't yet seen any value in connecting with them.

When asked a bit more about his rules and approach to networking this is what he had to say:

"Anyone who wants to network with everyone is useless. They will never have strong relationships developed, except perhaps with other crazy open networkers, and no one needs a network with people that you do not know and can not count on. Basically I have created a network of people willing to buy me drinks and kill for me in England and Australia. I just have to activate them.

In the USA, I follow a few basic rules:

- *No competitors in my network ever. If someone moves to a competitor, they are out of my network*
- *I allow everyone to see my connections if they are connected with me. If they do not do the same, I disconnect.*
- *I connect if I get a personal note. The standard "I'd like to connect with you on LinkedIn" does not get a response*

- *I don't connect with recruiters- They want to see who I know and worked with- they do not want to see me. I am unrecruitable. (New word!)*
- *If I would not recognize them in a store if they walked by me (and they are in my immediate community- Milwaukee WI), I will not connect.*
- *I do not connect with my team members, since I already have a connection there. I do connect with former team members"*

In short, being engaging and real on LinkedIn was the core message that Art was making. He went on to explain that he worked his way through college as a professional comedian. He was keen to point out that being funny is hard and not everyone is good at it. In Art's own words "It's weird not everyone is funny" and "Don't try to be funny if you haven't got it".

Overall I love the approach that Art has taken (and I agree with him it won't work for everyone). But everyone can learn something about their profile by thinking about the key points Art raises and his reasons and thoughts for doing this. The results speak for themselves; Art's profile has had a huge impact both online (in an outside of LinkedIn) and offline in the face to face world and that is something we think is just brilliant. I know this approach won't work for many (if any at all) and I know that some people will dislike Art's approach and be turned off. I find his humour, honesty and friendly approach engaging in a world full of spam bots, false profiles and automated responses. Art put the human and humorous approach back into business and like the man said "life is too short not to have fun". I look forward to buying you that drink Art.

As a footnote:

I asked Art to review the material for the book and check he was happy with what I had written about him.

His typical Art response below provides a nice little summary of his approach:

"The stuff you wrote about me is probably too nice. It is accurate and of course I like it. I always envisioned that an article written about me would be more of a police report, kind of dry, just reporting the facts of my unusual and surprisingly quick demise.

Remember the guy who was President of Segway? He drove his Segway off a cliff and died? And no one knew if it was an accident or on purpose? I kind of was hoping for that type of article. Without the dead part.

Perhaps someday you will get to update this book and wonder about what happened to Art Flater? He was a fabulously wealthy international celebrity who rose to fame on the strength of his linked in page and then one day disappeared like a James Bond villain, along with 3 or 4 international swimsuit supermodels. Or perhaps by that time, you will be part of the entourage, and you will not update the book, because you will be in the small group. Check with your wife to see if that would be OK.

It could happen.

Thanks you for all of the kind words. Don't forget to send me a copy of the book!"

Appendix 2

Bringing it all together (all the small things)

Let's be honest, these are all of the little snippets that are really useful to know and use, but don't quite fit in any of the other chapters of the book. This is a little bit of value add (it would have been easy to use this content elsewhere, but since you took the time to buy the book, hey, what the hell have this extra stuff for free!).

Paying for LinkedIn

We often get asked about paid options and spending money on LinkedIn and here are my thoughts on the current paid options on LinkedIn.

Paid options

There are a whole range of paid options for subscribing to the full LinkedIn service. Options range from just over £10 ($9.99) right the way through to nearly £500 ($549.99). LinkedIn offer you options in the following categories:

- LinkedIn Premium
- For Recruiters
- For Job Seekers
- For Sales Professionals

All of those have individual options within them, ranging from a basic paid for account right the way through to the full blown paid option within each area.

The main benefits of upgrading are:

InMail – this is the ability to send a direct message to anyone on LinkedIn without being connected to them. This can be very useful when targeting a specific sector. The quality of your InMail message is paramount here. It is a cold message from someone they (potentially) haven't heard of. Your message needs to be compelling enough for them to take note and do something about it. This is the equivalent of a cold call in the real (rather than online) world. I know one of our local companies, who organise local exhibitions, have had great results when attracting keynote speakers to their events. They have sent a direct InMail and have managed to secure some speakers directly rather than trying to track them down via websites etc.

More search results – get more information back and more results for your searches. This is very useful when assessing market size or doing some very specific search work in large groups of potential contacts or customers. On the basic version you are restricted to just the first 100 search results (more than enough for most folks) if you need more than this you need to get very good with advanced search or consider the paid options. If you think about the work we developed in Chapter 7, sometimes having access to a full list of search results is very useful.

See all of the people who have viewed your profile – as a basic user you can see the last 5 people who viewed you profile. If you are a popular person and have lots of views (or don't log in regularly) it is worth considering the upgrade. It is fascinating seeing who is looking at your profile and is a great source of new connections.

Advertising – you are able to advertise your products and services directly on LinkedIn. We have found this to be a very useful tool in targeting specific groups with specific products or services. Again this is an area where LinkedIn's own help centre is very good at assisting you in setting up your adverts. In essence, you create a very simple advert, with a picture and a small description of what you are advertising. You can then link this to your website with full details of what you offer. You can also offer the option that allows people who click on the advert to request more information, allowing you to contact them directly (with InMail even if you aren't connected to them). Our experience shows that this is very good in terms of getting your brand and specific adverts in front of a wide range of prospects. You pay for each "click" on your advert and LinkedIn allows you to set a daily limit on how much you spend on this. You are also able to select key parts to how the advert is displayed. You can choose the geographical area of the profiles who will see your advert. You can select the specific job roles and industries that you want to target. Advertising is a powerful targeted tool on LinkedIn, where a traditional online advert might not be targeted, on LinkedIn you can very specifically target the group that you want to see your adverts.

Sponsorship – this allows you to raise the profile of the information that you share either by your company or individual page. This is a powerful tool when it comes to the ideas around "thought leadership" and the concepts of inbound marketing. Sponsoring your updates gets you more coverage (i.e. more people see them) and can raise your profile with new groups. Where you are generating lots of useful and engaging content you can use sponsorship to reach a wider audience in a shorter space of time.

Tools to manage your LinkedIn account – these are the tools and software that sit outside of LinkedIn that may help make your work on LinkedIn a little easier. It is worth noting that LinkedIn regularly changes the way that external tools interact with it as a service, so some areas have stopped working or changed the way they work with LinkedIn. A good example of this was when LinkedIn stopped using apps and plugins to the main site. This disabled some useful functionality for users but LinkedIn has replaced this with its own versions, for example the videos shown on your profile used to be done via an app; you now do this as part of your main LinkedIn profile. So with that in mind – let's look at some of the key tools that work well with LinkedIn:

Hootsuite – this is a great tool for managing your social media (not just LinkedIn) accounts. Specifically for LinkedIn, you can schedule updates to go out on both your personal and LinkedIn company page. This helps enormously when you are short of time (that's pretty much all of us I think!). You can invest some time and find six or eight really useful articles you want to share with your company page followers or contacts on LinkedIn. If you don't use a tool that schedules your updates then these go out in one burst of activity. With Hootsuite you can schedule these updates to go out, one per day for the next six to eight days. This spreads the effect of the information and puts you in front of a wider audience by capturing different people at different times. It also generates the activity on LinkedIn that helps to raise your profile with others.

LinkedIn Sales Navigator tool – this is a premium service that LinkedIn aims straight at sales team of medium enterprises and larger. The main features you can use with this account are:

- The ability to use premium search filters to narrow down search results. This can be useful when focussing on suspects and prospects.
- Lead builder tool that gives you the ability to save key searches and lists you can build up through your activity on LinkedIn.
- Increased search results, 1000 search results versus the 100 in the standard free account.
- Use InMail's to directly contact those outside of your immediate network.

- Use the introduction tool to get access to your first degree contacts' own contacts.
- You will automatically get the LinkedIn OpenLink network so anyone on LinkedIn will be able to contact you directly.
- See full profiles across all of your network.
- Use TeamLink to identity your team member's connections in case they have an easier route any particular contact.
- Unlock the full list of who has viewed my profile.

We have addressed virtually all of these areas previously, so I won't go into detail here, other than to say if you do a significant amount of work on LinkedIn and have a reasonable size sales team (at least 10+) this is something you may want to consider.

There are a number of third party organisations offering significant 'plug in' to support larger clients and their teams using LinkedIn. Rather than provide a list (they do go out of date so quickly) have a look at your favourite search engine and I am sure you can find lists of organisations waiting to support you. Some of these tools will allow you to see a dashboard view of your employees' activity and engagement, as well as measure the effectiveness of the updates and information you share.

Customer Relationship Management (CRM) tools – These are the third party, often web based, pieces of software that allow you to effectively manage your sales process from suspect to advocate (see the sales cycle described in chapter 4). These tools, such as Sage Act, Microsoft Dynamics, Salesforce or simpler versions like Capsule, are great examples of powerful CRM systems. A lot of these tools link directly to LinkedIn to gather information and put it in one place. Think about this from your perspective first, others may well have you in their own CRM and it is pulling in your photo and key information from your profile. All the more reason for making sure that your profile is as good as it can be. We use a CRM tool that links to all of the great information on our suspects, prospects and customers on LinkedIn. This means all of the other work we do on LinkedIn isn't lost or forgotten when we use our CRM for customer interactions.

PROFILE CHECKLIST

Your LinkedIn check list	✓
Photo – does it represent you?	
Current Role – is it correct? Remember to use keywords	

Contact Information- is it all there and correct?
 	
  ○ Email address
  ○ Phone number
  ○ Twitter
  ○ Websites(s)
  ○ Facebook
  ○ Blog link
  ○ Address
	✓

Summary – what are you good at that will add value to other people's business?	
Experience – share your achievements	

Don't forget to send me your personalised connection requests. I love to hear from people and hear about how they have applied the information in this book. If you find new techniques or ways of applying the framework we have laid out, then please get in contact. We love to have discussions about improving things.

Enjoy using LinkedIn and getting the full benefits from using it as a powerful business tool.

About the Author

Nevil was involved with the UK launch of two familiar brands in Dyson and BlackBerry. He has worked as part of FTSE100 companies' management teams for over a decade and in sales for 25 years. Working at a major UK Telecoms and IT company, Nevil designed, launched and lead a new sales coaching programme for over 400 colleagues from General Manager to front line salespeople and this programme is still in place and being used to great effect. Nevil is an avid LinkedIn user, being a member of LinkedIn for the last 7 years. He was in the top 1% of searched profiles in 2012.

Nevil is a founding director of New Results Training Ltd a company delivering training in sales and management development as well as coaching individuals and helping organisations with their business strategy.

In Nevil's experience sales has always been seen as the poor relative in business terms than, say, marketing. One of his goals in life is to raise the professional standards of selling and get a message out to the business community that sales is a great, professional and rewarding career to be in.

By sharing his own journey, methods and approach, Nevil has helped countless business people go from good to great and progress on their own successful sales careers. Nevil has been at the sharp end of sales and the depth and breadth of his experience makes his training, coaching and seminars come to life, inspiring and motivating his audience. Nevil's blend of theory and his own personal experience helps his audiences connect their own ideas and find their own paths.

Lightning Source UK Ltd.
Milton Keynes UK
UKOW01f0557051016

284470UK00001B/11/P